Great Essays

An Introduction to Writing Essays

Second Edition

Keith S. Folse
University of Central Florida

April Muchmore-Vokoun
University of South Florida

Elena Vestri Solomon
Hillsborough Community College

Houghton Mifflin Company
Boston New York

Publisher: Patricia A. Coryell
Director of ESL Publishing: Susan Maguire
Senior Development Editor: Kathy Sands-Boehmer
Development Editor: Kathleen M. Smith
Editorial Assistant: Evangeline Bermas
Senior Project Editor: Tracy Patruno
Manufacturing Manager: Florence Cadran
Marketing Manager: Annamarie Rice

Cover Image: Colorful Interlocking Gears, ©2002 The Studio Dog/Gettyone

Printed in the U.S.A.

Library of Congress Control Number: 2003106680

ISBN: 0-618-27191-0

123456789-B-07 06 05 04 03

Contents

Unit 2 Narrative Essays   37

Unit 3 Comparison Essays   63

Unit 4 Cause-Effect Essays   86

Unit 5 Argumentative Essays 109

Appendixes   129

Overview

Great Essays gives introductory instruction and extensive practical exercises and activities in essay writing at the high-intermediate and advanced levels. This book contains a wide variety of exercises that offer practice in both working with the writing process and developing a final written product. We assume that students can write good paragraphs and that what they need is instruction in, modeling of, and guidance with essays.

There are as many ways to write essays as there are writers. Essay writing reflects a writer's knowledge of essay conventions as much as it reflects the writer's creativity. Thus, essay writing is both a science and an art. Since no art form can be "taught" precisely, this book offers models of good academic essays as the basic level of essay writing from which students produce their own essays. We realize that some students may not go beyond the level of the examples whereas other students may advance in their essay writing.

In *Great Essays* we have made a conscious effort to include a wide array of writing activities representing varying approaches to the teaching of writing. Although we realize that few writing teachers are completely satisfied with any writing text, we believe that within this wide variety of activities and approaches, most teachers will find what their students need in order to improve writing skills, presented in a way that is compatible with how teachers think ESL writing ought to be taught.

We have made every effort to include more than enough writing instruction and practice to eliminate the need for excessive ancillary materials. The textbook contains sixty-three activities with twenty-five suggestions for additional essay writing assignments. In addition, the text has appendixes with supplementary practice in language usage and grammar. Most of these activities and practice exercises are based on the twenty-five full-length essays found throughout the text.

We designed this book for high-intermediate to advanced students. Depending on the class level and the amount of writing that is done outside of class hours, there is enough material for sixty-to-eighty classroom hours. Provided that enough writing is done outside of the classroom, the number of hours can be as little as forty.

Some ESL students are already good writers in their native language. *Great Essays* will allow these students to study the different rhetorical styles commonly used in English writing. Other students need work in the basic steps involved in the process of composing an essay. These students in particular will benefit from the step-by-step activities in *Great Essays*.

Composing an essay involves both a process and a product. All ESL students are rightfully concerned about their written products. For many students, not being able to write effectively and easily in English is a major obstacle to their educational plans. Thus, the quality of any written work is important. To this end, the activities in this book deal with elements that affect the quality of a written product, including grammar, organization, and logic. Though in this text there is information about both process and product in essay writing, it should be noted that the focus is slightly more on the final written product.

The best judge of which units and which activities should be covered with any group of students is always the teacher. It is up to you to gauge the needs of your students and then match these needs with the material in this book.

TEXT ORGANIZATION

Great Essays consists of two general sections. The first section consists of the five actual units that present the features of a good essay and four kinds of essay writing. The second section includes six appendixes: a description of the steps in the writing process, sentence-combining activities, sentence types, grammar practice, information about connectors, and peer editing sheets.

UNITS 1–5

This section begins by teaching, in general terms, how to construct a good essay. The first unit presents the overall organization of an essay. It also offers some specific suggestions for writing the introduction of the essay, including how to write a good hook and a solid thesis statement. Students who are already familiar with the essay form may skip most of the material in Unit 1. Units 2 to 5 teach four different kinds of essays. They are narrative, comparison, cause-effect, and argumentative. These four essay types can be covered in any order.

APPENDIXES

This section consists of six appendixes. Appendix 1 explains the seven steps in the process of writing an essay and includes student examples for a few of the steps.

Appendix 2, new to the second edition, is dedicated to sentence-combining skills. Individual sentences taken from each of the sample essays have been isolated and divided into short, choppy sentences that students are asked to combine into longer sentences. This type of activity exercises students' skills in using prepositional phrases, coordinating conjunctions, conjunctive adverbs, and other transitional devices to write concise sentences. After completing the exercises, students are able to check their written products with the original sentences found in the example essays.

Appendix 3, also new to this edition, complements Appendix 2 by defining the three basic sentence types in English and giving examples and practice.

Appendix 4 has additional grammar activities in the context of paragraphs within whole essays. Many ESL students see grammar as their biggest problem. While other writing needs often deserve more attention, students recognize that their ability to express themselves in English is limited by the level of their English proficiency. To help with some of the most common grammar problems, Appendix 4 contains practice exercises.

Appendix 5 contains a list of useful connectors, supplementing the Language Focus sections that feature connectors in the units.

In Appendix 6 you will find peer editing sheets for students to use when they read each other's work and offer feedback. For each essay type, there is a peer editing sheet for the outline and another for the essay. We believe that asking a student to comment on another student's writing without guidance is poor pedagogy and may result in hurt feelings for the writer. Not everyone is a good writer; therefore, we cannot assume that a less capable writer is able to make useful comments on a better writer's paper. Likewise, not all good writers know how to guide weaker writers toward an improved essay. These peer editing sheets provide focused guidance to help everyone make useful comments. For those students who are able to go beyond the basics, several of the questions are open-ended and invite additional comments.

CONTENTS OF A UNIT

Following are the common features of each unit. Though each unit has a specific writing goal and language focus (listed at the beginning of the unit), the following features appear in every unit.

EXAMPLE ESSAYS

Because we believe that writing and reading are inextricably related, the example essays are often preceded by short schema-building questions for small groups or the whole class. Potentially unfamiliar vocabulary is underlined in the essay and defined after it. Example essays are usually followed by questions specifically constructed to focus learners' attention on organization, syntactic structures, or other essay features.

WRITER'S NOTES

Rather than large boxed areas overflowing with information, *Great Essays* features small chunks of writing advice under this heading. The content of these notes varies greatly from brainstorming techniques to peer editing guidelines to hints for generating supporting details.

LANGUAGE FOCUS

This section focuses students' attention on word-level details that we believe are important to the kind of essay featured in the unit. If students work with different writing devices, such as connectors, they will be better equipped to use them in their own writing. Those students who need more practice should work through any related additional practices in Appendix 4.

BUILDING BETTER SENTENCES

After every example essay read, students are asked to turn to Appendix 2 and work on building better sentences. This activity focuses on students' sentence-level writing skills. For those students who lack confidence in producing longer or more complicated sentences, this type of activity concentrates on the manipulation of words and ideas on the sentence level.

COMPLETING AN OUTLINE

In each unit, students are asked to read partial outlines and fill in the missing pieces. This strategy will help develop students' organizational skills in providing appropriate supporting details and in organizing ideas within an essay.

COMPLETING A SAMPLE ESSAY

In Units 2 to 5, students are asked to fill in the missing supporting details in a partial essay, which is a reinforcement of the model presented earlier in the unit. We designed this activity to give further practice in writing supporting sentences in paragraphs.

ANALYZING AN ESSAY

For each essay type, students using *Great Essays* are asked to read an essay and answer questions that focus on various aspects of writing at the high-intermediate to advanced levels, for example, recognizing the topic sentence, identifying the use of examples as support, or discovering the writer's purpose for including certain information.

TOPICS FOR WRITING

Each unit ends with an assignment to write an essay in the rhetorical style covered in the unit. For further practice, we include a list of five additional writing ideas in each unit.

PEER EDITING

In these activities in each unit, student partners offer each other written comments with the goal of improving their essays. Just as students have different writing abilities, so also do they have different editing abilities. For this reason, we believe that students benefit from *guided* peer editing. After students write an outline, they can use the peer editing sheet for outlines, which addresses content and organization. Students can receive valuable advice from each other regarding thesis statements, topic sentences, supporting information, and logic before writing the essay. The second peer editing activity is for the essay. Pairs of students exchange their completed essays and offer written comments, using the peer editing sheet. We recommend that students spend fifteen-to-twenty minutes reading a classmate's essay and writing comments according to the questions on the peer editing sheet. Since a certain amount of trust and cooperation is involved in peer editing, it is important to make sure that students work with peers that they feel compatible with.

EXTRA PRACTICE ACTIVITIES

Students using *Great Essays* are encouraged to visit the Houghton Mifflin website (http://esl.college.hmco.com/students) for additional practice in writing. Instructors can access the Answer Key at the password-protected website (http://esl.college.hmco.com/instructors).

ABOUT THE ACTIVITIES AND PRACTICES

Teachers have long noticed that students often do well with grammar in discrete sentences but may have problems with the same grammar when it occurs in an essay. Consequently, most of the activities and practices in *Great Essays* work with complete essays or focus on one paragraph within an essay. For example, instead of several unrelated sentences for practice with connectors, there is a complete essay. Our hope is that by practicing the grammatical problem in the target medium, students will produce more accurate writing sooner.

The earliest ESL composition textbooks were merely extensions of ESL grammar classes. The activities in these books did not practice English composition as much as they did ESL grammar points. Later books, on the other hand, tended to focus too much on the composing process. We feel that this focus ignores the important fact that the real goals of our ESL students are both to produce a presentable product and to master the composing process. From our years of ESL and other L2 teaching experience, we believe that *Great Essays* allows ESL students to achieve both of these goals.

On the Web

For the answer key, additional exercises, and other instuctor resources, visit the *Great Essays* instructor website at

http://esl.college.hmco.com/instructors

Additional exercises for each unit are available to students on the *Great Essays* student website at

http://esl.college.hmco.com/students

ACKNOWLEDGMENTS

We would like to thank ESL and English composition colleagues who generously shared their ideas, insights, and feedback on L2 writing, university English course requirements, and textbook design. In addition, we would like to thank teachers on two electronic lists, TESL-L and TESLIE-L, who responded to our queries and thereby helped us write this book.

We would also like to thank our editors at Houghton Mifflin, Susan Maguire and Kathy Sands Boehmer, and our development editor, Kathleen Smith, for their indispensable guidance throughout the birth and growth of this project. We are grateful to Joann Kozyrev and Anna Rice at Houghton Mifflin for their enthusiastic support of our works.

Likewise, we are indebted to the following reviewers who offered ideas and suggestions that shaped our revisions:

Don Beck, University of Findlay, OH

Len Chen, Palomar College, CA

Pauline Chu, Long Island Business Institute, NY

Gretchen Mack, Community College of Denver, CO

Nick Hilmers, DePaul University, IL

Gloria Huang, DePaul University, IL

Danielle Pelletier, Northeastern University, MA

Christine Tierney, Houston Community College, TX

Finally, many thanks go to our students who have taught us what ESL composition ought to be. Without them, this work would have been impossible.

Keith S. Folse

April Muchmore-Vokoun

Elena Vestri Solomon

Great Essays

Exploring the Essay

UNIT 1

GOAL: To learn about the structure of an essay

WHAT IS AN ESSAY?

Essays are everywhere—in books, magazines, newspapers, and other printed material. An essay is a short collection of paragraphs that presents facts, opinions, and ideas on a topic. Topics can range from a description of a visit to Disney World to an argument about capital punishment.

An essay usually has three to ten paragraphs. Most of the essays in this book have five or six paragraphs. Each paragraph discusses one idea, often stated in the topic sentence of the paragraph. This idea is related to the topic of the whole essay. The topic sentence of a paragraph can be located anywhere, but the most common place is at the beginning of the paragraph.

The following illustration shows how letters, words, sentences, paragraphs, and essays are related. Letters can be combined into a word. Words can be combined into a sentence. Sentences can be combined into a paragraph. Finally, paragraphs can be combined into an essay. In this book, you will study essays.

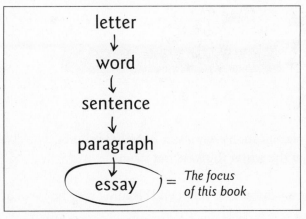

letter
↓
word
↓
sentence
↓
paragraph
↓
essay) = *The focus of this book*

Connections

1

KINDS OF ESSAYS

There are many different ways to write an essay. The method that a writer chooses is based on the topic of the essay and the kind of essay that presents the topic in the best way. For example, in an essay that compares the lifestyles of actors and professional athletes, the writer would use a comparison format.

In this book, you will learn about four common kinds of essays: narrative, comparison, cause-effect, and argumentative. Each of the next four units presents one of these kinds of essay writing. However, it is important to note here that most writers use more than one method. For example, if you are comparing the lifestyles of actors and professional athletes, you might include information about how actors and professional athletes get their start in their careers (cause-effect). You might also give an account of a specific athlete's story (narrative). In addition, your essay could include facts and opinions about how one profession is more respected than the other (argumentative).

It is likely that a good writer will use more than one kind of writing in an essay. Once you learn about these essay methods separately and become comfortable with them, you can experiment with weaving them together to produce well-written essays in English.

On the Web
Try Unit 1
Activity 1

WRITER'S NOTE: Parts of an Essay

Notice that an essay always has three basic parts: the **introduction,** the **body,** and the **conclusion.** The introduction is the first paragraph, the conclusion is the last paragraph, and the body consists of the paragraphs in between. You will study these three parts later in this unit.

EXAMPLE ESSAYS

Read and study these five example essays. Work with a partner to answer the questions before and after the essays. These questions will help you understand the content and the organization of the essays.

Activity 1   Studying an Example Essay

Essay 1

This is a classification essay about household chores. The essay lists typical chores and explains what the writer thinks about them.

1. How much time do you spend cleaning your house or apartment each week?
2. What is your least favorite household chore? Why?

EXAMPLE ESSAY

Cinderella and Her <u>Odious</u> <u>Household</u> <u>Chores</u>

1 Everyone knows how the story of Cinderella ends, but did you ever really think about how she spent her days before she met the prince? Her daily routine was not glamorous. She did everything from sweeping the floor to cooking the meals. If someone had asked Cinderella, "Are there any household chores that you particularly hate?" she probably would have answered, "Why, none, of course. Housework is my duty!" In the real world, however, most people have definite dislikes for certain household chores. The top three of these tasks include ironing clothes, washing dishes, and cleaning the bathroom.

2 One of the most hated chores for many people is ironing clothes because it is not a task that can be completed quickly or thoughtlessly. Each piece of clothing must be handled individually, so ironing a basket of laundry can take hours! After ironing a piece of clothing <u>meticulously</u>, which entails smoothing out the fabric, following the seams, and getting the creases "just right," it needs to be put on a hanger as soon as possible. If not, this item might become wrinkled and need to be ironed again. Perhaps that is why ironing is not a favorite chore. It requires extreme attention to detail from beginning to end.

3 Another household chore that many people dislike is washing dishes. Of course, some people claim that this chore is no longer a problem because dishwashers are available now! However, no one would argue that dishes, <u>silverware</u>, and especially pots and pans washed in a dishwasher come out as clean as they do when washed by hand. For this reason, many people continue to wash their dishes by hand, but they are not necessarily happy doing it. Washing dishes is a dirty job that requires not only the <u>elbow grease</u> to scrape food off the dishes but also the patience to rinse and dry them. In addition, unlike ironing clothes, washing dishes is a chore that usually must be done every day. Regardless of how Cinderella felt about this particular chore, it is obvious that most people do not enjoy doing it.

4 Though ironing clothes and washing dishes are not the most pleasant household chores, perhaps the most dreaded is cleaning the bathroom. This involves <u>tackling</u> three main areas: the bathtub, sink, and toilet. Because the bathroom is full of germs, a quick wiping of the surfaces is not enough. As a result, strong bathroom cleansers are

ESSAY

necessary to clean and <u>disinfect</u> this room. The task of cleaning the bathroom is so unpleasant that some people wear rubber gloves when they attempt it. The only positive point about cleaning the bathroom is that it does not have to be done on a daily basis.

5   Maintaining a house means doing a wide variety of unpleasant chores. Cinderella knew this, and so do we. Many of us do not have the luxury of hiring an outside person to do our housework, so we must make do with our responsibilities. If we can take pride in the results of our hard work, maybe we can get through the unpleasantness of these typical household chores.

odious: very unpleasant

household: referring to the house

chore: a specific task or job

meticulously: thoroughly and carefully

silverware: eating utensils; forks, knives, and spoons

elbow grease: physical strength, usually using the hands

tackling: undertaking, beginning

disinfect: purify; eliminate germs

3. According to the author of this essay, what are the three least popular household chores?

_____   _____   _____

WRITER'S NOTE: The Hook

The opening sentence of any essay is called the **hook.** A hook in writing is used to "catch" readers and get their interest so that they will want to read the essay. (See pages 21–23 for more information about hooks.)

4. In a few words, describe the hook of this essay. _____

_____

5. Do you think this hook is effective? Does it grab your attention? Why, or why not?

_____

_____

6. How many paragraphs does this essay have? _____ Which paragraph is the introduction?

_____ the conclusion? _____ Which paragraphs are the body? _____

7. In a few words, what is the general topic of this essay? _____

_____

WRITER'S NOTE: The Thesis Statement

In "Cinderella and Her Odious Household Chores," the last sentence in paragraph 1 is the **thesis statement.** It states the main idea of the essay and tells what the organization of the information will be. (See page 24 for more information about thesis statements.)

8. Can you find a sentence in paragraph 1 that tells readers what to expect in paragraphs 2, 3, and 4?

   Write that sentence here. _____

   _____

9. What is the main idea of paragraph 2? _____

   _____

   Can you find one sentence that introduces this topic? Write it here.

   _____

   _____

   _____

WRITER'S NOTE: The Topic Sentence

Every good paragraph has a **topic sentence.** The topic sentence tells the reader the main topic of the paragraph. Sometimes it also gives the reader a hint about the writer's purpose.

10. Write the topic sentences of paragraph 3 and paragraph 4.

   Paragraph 3: _____

   _____

   _____

   _____

Paragraph 4: _____

_____

_____

_____

WRITER'S NOTE: Supporting Sentences

The **supporting sentences** in an essay are in the body. (See pages 30–34 for information about the body.) Supporting sentences always relate to the topic sentence of the paragraph in which they occur. Common supporting sentences give examples, reasons, facts, or more specific information. Without supporting sentences, an essay would be nothing more than a general outline.

11. Supporting sentences: In paragraph 2, the writer shows that people do not like to iron clothes. Write two of the supporting sentences here.

_____

_____

_____

12. Supporting sentences: In paragraph 4, the writer suggests that cleaning the bathroom is not a simple or fast chore. Write the sentence in which the writer makes this point.

_____

_____

_____

WRITER'S NOTE: The Conclusion

It is important for an essay to have a good **conclusion.** Notice that the writer mentions Cinderella again in the last paragraph of "Cinderella and Her Odious Household Chores." The introduction and the conclusion often share some ideas and words. (See pages 35–36 for more information about writing the conclusion of an essay.)

13. Look at the last paragraph. Find the sentence that restates the thesis. Write that sentence here.

_____

_____

_____

Building Better Sentences

Correct and varied sentence structure is essential to the quality of your essay. For further practice with "Cinderella and Her Odious Household Chores," go to Practice 1 on page 142 in Appendix 2.

Activity 2   **Studying an Example Essay**

Essay 2

In this narrative essay, the writer tells a story of a humorous language problem he experienced in Japan.

1. What are some words that cause problems for you in English? Why are they difficult?

2. Describe a situation in which you could not express yourself effectively in English. What did you do?

EXAMPLE ESSAY

How Do You Say . . . ?

1   What would happen if you woke up one day and suddenly found yourself in a world where you could not communicate with anyone? I am a teacher of English as a second language (ESL). In June 1988, I accepted a job in a <u>rural</u> area of Japan called Niigata and found myself faced with this language problem. One event <u>in particular stands out</u> as an example of my inability to express my ideas to the people around me <u>due to</u> my <u>lack</u> of vocabulary.

2   I had been in Japan only a few days, and I was feeling restless. I wanted to make some fresh bread, so I <u>set out for</u> the store with the simple intention of buying some flour. I had taken some Japanese language classes before I arrived in Japan. Although I knew my Japanese skills were limited, my lack of knowledge did not stop me from going to the store to buy flour. I thought that I would locate the section where the grains were displayed and find the bag that had a picture of either bread or flour on it.

3   The small town where I lived had one tiny store. I wandered around the store a few times, but I did not see a bag of anything that appeared to be flour. In the United States, flour usually comes in a paper bag with pictures of biscuits or bread on it, so this is what I was looking for. I finally found a few clear plastic bags that had bread <u>crumbs</u>

inside, so I thought that flour might be located nearby. No matter how many bags I examined, I could not find any flour.

4   I desperately wanted to ask one of the three elderly women clerks where the flour was, but I could not do this simple task. I knew how to ask where something was, but I did not know the word for "flour." I tried to think of how to say "flour" using different words such as "white powder" or "the ingredient that you use to make bread," but I did not know "powder" and I did not know "ingredient." Just then, I saw one of my students leaving the store. I rushed outside to his car and explained that I needed to know a word in Japanese. "How do you say 'flour'?" I asked. He told me the word was *hana*.

5   I rushed back into the store, which was about to close for the evening. I found one of the elderly clerks and asked in my best Japanese, *"Sumimasen. Hana wa doko desu ka?"* or "Excuse me. Where is the *hana*?" The petite old woman said something in Japanese and raced to the far right side of the store. "Finally," I thought, "I am going to get my flour and go home to make bread." However, my hopes ended rather quickly when I followed the clerk to the produce section. I saw green onions, tomatoes, and even pumpkins, but I could not understand why flour would be there. The woman then pointed to the beautiful yellow chrysanthemums next to the green onions.

6   At first I was puzzled, but suddenly it all made sense. I had been in the country long enough to know that people in Japan eat chrysanthemums in salads. I was standing in front of the f-l-o-w-e-r display, not the f-l-o-u-r display. When I asked my student for the Japanese word for "flour," I did not specify whether I meant "flour" or "flower" because it had never occurred to me that grocery stores, especially small ones, might sell flowers.

7   I did not buy any chrysanthemums that night. I was not able to find the flour either. My lack of knowledge about Japanese cuisine and my very limited knowledge of Japanese caused me to go home empty-handed that night. However, I learned the often-underestimated value of simple vocabulary in speaking a second language. For me, this event in a small store in rural Japan really opened my eyes to my lack of vocabulary skills.

rural: of the countryside; the opposite of *urban*

in particular: especially

stand out: to be different from the other members of the group

due to: because of

lack: a shortage

set out for: to start going to a place

crumbs: tiny pieces of food

produce: fresh fruits and vegetables

pumpkin: a large, round, orange fruit

chrysanthemum: a type of flower

specify: to say exactly

3. In a few sentences, tell what happened in this story. Use your own words.

_____

_____

_____

_____

_____

_____

_____

4. A good hook in an essay sometimes involves the reader in what follows. Write the hook for this essay.

_____

_____

5. How does this hook try to involve the reader? Do you think that this hook is successful? Why, or why not?

_____

_____

_____

6. How many paragraphs are in this essay? _____ In which paragraph does the writer

reveal what the problem is with the question he asked in Japanese? _____

7. Supporting sentences: Why does the writer include the information in paragraph 6? (Hint: What supporting information does the writer give to explain the language miscommunication?)

_____

_____

8. This essay tells a story. It is an organized sequence of events. This kind of essay is called a **narrative essay** (Unit 2).

Here is a list of the main events in the essay. Read the list and number the items from 1 to 12 to indicate the order of the events.

_____ The clerk took the writer to the produce section.

_____ The writer asked the student for a Japanese translation.

_____ The clerk pointed to the flowers.

_____ The writer arrived in Japan.

_____ The writer wanted to make some bread.

_____ The writer spoke to an elderly clerk.

_____ The writer realized that the student had not understood the question correctly.

_____ The writer went home without the flour.

_____ The writer looked all over the store for the flour.

_____ The writer saw one of his students.

_____ The writer studied Japanese.

_____ The writer went to the store.

Building Better Sentences

Correct and varied sentence structure is essential to the quality of your essay. For further practice with "How Do You Say . . .?" go to Practice 2 on page 143 in Appendix 2.

Activity 3   **Studying an Example Essay**

Essay 3

Which do you like better, the city or the countryside? Read this comparison essay about some differences between these two types of places.

1. Describe the place where you grew up.
2. What were the best and worst things about living there?

The <u>Urban</u> and Rural Divide

EXAMPLE ESSAY

1 Imagine life in Los Angeles. Now imagine life in a neighboring rural California town. Finally, picture life in Cairo, Egypt. Which of these last two places is more different from Los Angeles? Many people might mistakenly choose Cairo because it is in a different country. In fact, city <u>dwellers</u> all over the world tend to have similar lifestyles, so the biggest differences are between Los Angeles and its smaller neighbor. Urban people and rural people, <u>regardless of</u> their country, live quite differently. Perhaps some of the most <u>notable</u> differences in the lives of these two groups include the <u>degree</u> of friendliness, the <u>pace</u> of life, and the variety of activities.

2 One major difference between growing up in the city and in the country is the degree of friendliness. In large cities, we often hear of people living in huge apartment buildings with hundreds of strangers. These urban apartment dwellers tend to be <u>wary</u> of unknown faces and rarely get to know their neighbors well. The situation in a small town is often just the opposite. Small-town people generally grow up together, attend the same schools and churches, and share the same friends. As a result, rural people are much more likely to treat their neighbors like family and invite them into their homes.

3 Another difference is the pace of life. In the city, life moves very quickly. The streets reflect this hectic pace and are rarely empty, even late at night. City dwellers appear to be racing to get somewhere important. Life for them tends to be a series of <u>deadlines</u>. In the country, life is much slower. Even during <u>peak</u> hours, traffic jams occur less often. Stores close in the early evening, and the streets do not come alive until the next

morning. The people here seem more relaxed and move in a more leisurely way. The pace of life in these two areas could not be more different.

4   A third difference lies in the way people are able to spend their free time. Although life in the city has its <u>drawbacks</u>, city dwellers have a much wider choice of activities that they can participate in. For example, they can go to museums, eat in exotic restaurants, attend concerts, and shop in hundreds of stores. The activities available to people in rural areas, however, are much more limited. It is rare to find museums or exotic restaurants there. Concert tours almost never include stops in country towns. Finally, people who enjoy shopping might be disappointed in the small number of stores.

5   Life in urban areas and life in rural areas vary in terms of human interaction, pace of life, and daily activities. Other important differences exist, too, but none of these makes one place better than the other. The places are simply different. Only people who have experienced living in both the city and the country can truly appreciate the unique characteristics of each.

urban: of the city

dwellers: those who live in a place

regardless of: in spite of

notable: important; worthy of notice

degree: amount

pace: speed; rate

wary: cautious, suspicious

deadline: the time limit for doing something

peak: the highest; the top (amount)

drawbacks: disadvantages, negative points

3. What is the topic of this essay?

_____

The writer's purpose is to compare and contrast life in two locations. This kind of essay is called a **comparison essay** (Unit 3).

4. What is the thesis statement? _____

_____

_____

5. In each paragraph, which location is always discussed first, rural or urban?

_____

6. Which paragraph talks about activities in each area? _____ Which place offers more

options for activities? _____

7. Supporting sentences: Some of the supporting sentences in "The Urban and Rural Divide" contrast the pace of life in the two areas. Write those sentences in the chart under the correct heading. Include the paragraph number.

Pace of Life (paragraph _____)

   A. Urban

      1. _____

      2. _____

      3. _____

      4. _____

   B. Rural

      1. _____

      2. _____

      3. _____

      4. _____

Building Better Sentences

Correct and varied sentence structure is essential to the quality of your essay. For further practice with "The Urban and Rural Divide," go to Practice 3 on Page 144 in Appendix 2.

Activity 4   **Studying an Example Essay**

Essay 4

This cause-effect essay tells about the connection between cancer and an unhealthy lifestyle.

1. Do you think people are healthier now than in the past? Why, or why not?

2. What three changes could you make in your lifestyle to become healthier? Be specific.

EXAMPLE ESSAY

Cancer Risks

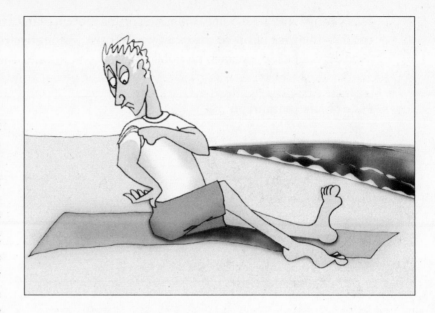

1 Lung cancer kills more people in one year than all criminal and accidental deaths combined. These statistics are shocking, but the good news is that people are now well-informed about the risks connected to lung cancer. They know that their risk of contracting this terrible disease decreases if they either stop smoking or do not smoke at all. Unfortunately, the same cannot be said about other types of cancer. Many people are not aware that their everyday behavior can lead to the development of these different forms of cancer. By eating better, exercising regularly, and staying out of the sun, people can reduce their risks.

2 Instead of foods that are good for them, people often eat hamburgers, cheese, French fries, and pizza. These common foods contain large amounts of saturated fat, which is the worst kind of fat. Though light and fat-free products are constantly being introduced to the consumer market, many people still buy food that contains fat because it often tastes better. However, eating fatty foods can increase a person's chances for some kinds of cancer. People do not eat as many fresh vegetables and fresh fruits as they used to. Instead, they now eat a lot more processed foods that do not contain natural <u>fiber</u>. Lack of fiber in a person's diet can increase the chance of <u>colon</u> cancer. In the past, people with less information about nutrition actually had better <u>diets</u> than people do today. They also had fewer cases of cancer.

3 Many people today are overweight, and being overweight has been connected to some kinds of cancer. This is the generation that started the couch potato boom, and today's couch potatoes are bigger than ever. Health experts warn that being overweight is a risk not only for heart disease but also for certain kinds of cancer. The best way to <u>attain</u> a healthy weight again is to <u>cut back on</u> the amount of food and to exercise regularly. It is not possible to do only one of these and lose weight permanently. The improved diet must be <u>in conjunction with</u> regular exercise. In the past, people did more physical activity than people do today. For example, people used to walk to work; now almost no one does. In addition, people had jobs that required more physical labor. Now many people have desk jobs in front of computers.

4 Finally, health officials are gravely concerned by the <u>astounding</u> rise in the cases of skin cancer. Many societies value a tanned complexion, so on weekends people tend to <u>flock to</u> the beach or swimming pools and lie in the sun. Many of these people do not use a safe sunscreen, and the result is that they often get sunburned. Sunburn damages the skin, and repeated damage may lead to skin cancer later in life. Once the damage is done, it cannot be undone. Thus, prevention is important. In the past, people did not lie in direct sunlight for long periods, and skin cancer was not as <u>prevalent</u> as it is now. People have started to listen to doctors' warnings about this situation, and more and more people are using proper sunscreens. Unfortunately, millions of people already have this potential cancer problem in their skin and may develop cancer later.

ESSAY

5 Cancer has been around since the earliest days of human existence, but only recently has the public been made aware of some of the risk factors involved. Anti-smoking campaigns can be seen everywhere: on billboards, television, radio, and newsprint. If the same amount of attention were given to proper diets, exercise, and sunscreens, perhaps the number of overall cancer cases would be reduced.

fiber: a plant material that is good for the digestive system

colon: an organ in the digestive system

diet: a special plan for losing weight; what a person eats

attain: to achieve

cut back on: to reduce the amount (of something)

in conjunction with: at the same time as; together with

astounding: amazing; surprising

flock to: to go to a place in large numbers (as birds do)

prevalent: common

3. What is the writer's main message in this essay? _____

_____

_____

The writer presents several causes for the rise in the number of cancer cases. This kind of organization is called a **cause-effect essay** (Unit 4). In this kind of essay, the writer shows that one thing happened (effect) because something else happened first (cause).

4. What is the thesis statement of the essay?

_____

_____

5. The thesis statement should tell the reader how the paper will be organized. What do you know about the organization of the essay from the thesis statement?

_____

_____

6. Supporting sentences: In paragraph 2, the writer states that many people eat unhealthy food. What supporting information explains why this food is not healthy?

_____

_____

7. Supporting sentences: The writer also explains why people enjoy eating unhealthy food. Write the reason here.

_____

Building Better Sentences

Correct and varied sentence structure is essential to the quality of your essay. For further practice with "Cancer Risks," go to Practice 4 on page 145 in Appendix 2.

| Activity 5 | **Studying an Example Essay** |

Essay 5

Choosing a college is an important decision. This essay may help you decide.

1. What do you know about community colleges? How are they different from universities?

2. What are some things that students consider when they are choosing a college?

An Alternative to University Education

ESSAY

1   A high school diploma is not the end of many people's education these days. High school students who want to continue their education generally choose one of two routes after graduation. Some students <u>opt to</u> attend a community college and then transfer to a university, while others go directly to a university. Making this difficult choice requires a great deal of careful thought. However, if the choice is based on three specific factors, <u>namely</u>, cost, location, and quality of education, students will quickly see the advantages that attending a community college offers.

EXAMPLE ESSAY

2   Attending a community college is much cheaper than attending a university. For example, <u>tuition</u> at a local community college I attended might cost less than $3,000 for two years. The same classes taken at a nearby university would cost almost $5,000. In addition, a university would charge more for parking, photocopying at the library, cafeteria food, campus health clinic services, and textbooks. No matter how the total bill is calculated or what is included, it is more expensive to study at a university.

3   Attending a community college can be more convenient because of its location. Going to a university often requires recent high school graduates to live far from home, and many of them are <u>reluctant</u> to do so. These students are only seventeen or eighteen years old and may have very little experience at being away from home. It would be difficult for these young people to suddenly find themselves far away from their families. In addition, very few parents are prepared to send their teenagers to distant universities. Because almost every area has a community college, students who opt to go to a community college can continue to be near their families for two more years.

4   Finally, there are educational benefits to attending a community college. University life is very different from community college life. A university campus offers a large variety of sports events and parties, and students can easily become distracted from their studies. Community colleges, which typically have fewer students and extracurricular activities, may be a better environment for serious study. In addition, the library facilities at a community college, though not as large as those at a university, are more than sufficient for the kind of work that is required in first- or second-year courses. Class size is also an issue to consider. Introductory courses at universities often have fifty to sixty or even one hundred students. In such large classes, student-teacher interaction usually is minimal, and learning can be more difficult for some students. Finally, the teaching at community colleges is often better than the teaching at a university. Professors at community colleges have the same credentials as those at universities, and community college professors spend most of their time teaching instead of conducting research, as university professors have to do.

5   The decision to enter a university directly or to attend a community college for the first two years after high school can be difficult. Community colleges are not as glamorous as large universities. They are often seen as second-rate alternatives to the more-well known universities. However, based on the three important factors outlined above—cost, location, and quality of education—it is clear that for many students, choosing a community college is the smarter thing to do.

opt to: to choose to (do something)	**reluctant:** hesitant
namely: such as; for example	**minimal:** the least possible
tuition: money paid for classes	**credentials:** qualifications

3. What two things are being compared in this essay?

_____

Which one does the writer think is better?

_____

_____

In essays like this one, the writer is comparing or contrasting two or more things. However, unlike "The Urban and Rural Divide" (Essay 3, page 11), in "An Alternative to University Education," the writer compares community colleges and universities with the intention of persuading the reader to agree that community colleges are better for new high school graduates. This kind of essay is called an **argumentative essay** (Unit 5). Some books call this a persuasive essay.

4. What is the organization of this essay? Fill in the blanks of this simple outline with the words that are missing.

TOPIC: The Advantages of Community Colleges

Paragraph 1: Introduction

Thesis statement: _____

_____

Paragraph 2 topic: _____

A. Community college cost: $ _____

B. _____ : $ _____

C. Other higher university costs

1. Parking

2. _____

3. _____

4. Health clinic services

5. _____

SUPPORT

Paragraph 3 topic: Location

SUPPORT

    A. Students' reasons

    B. _____

    _____

Paragraph 4 topic: _____

SUPPORT

    A. Quiet campus

    B. _____

    C. Class size

    D. Quality of teaching

Paragraph 5: Conclusion

5. The writer discusses three factors—cost, location, and quality of education—in the decision about what kind of college to attend. Can you think of two other factors that the writer could have used?

_____

_____

6. Before you read this essay, did you know much about this topic? What was your opinion before you read this essay? (Check all possible answers.)

_____ I thought that attending a university directly after high school was best.

_____ I thought that attending a community college after high school was best.

_____ I thought that a university offered a better education than a community college.

_____ I thought that a community college offered a better education than a university.

_____ I thought that a university was cheaper than a community college.

_____ I thought that a community college was cheaper than a university.

_____ I did not know much about university education in the United States.

_____ I did not know much about community college education in the United States.

7. Did your opinion about community colleges change after you read "An Alternative to University Education"? In other words, did the writer persuade you to change your mind about community

   colleges in the United States? _____

8. Which part of the essay was the most persuasive for you?

   _____

   _____

9. If your answer to question 7 is "yes," tell why your opinion changed. If your answer to question 7 is "no," write three specific reasons why you believe a university is a better choice.

   _____

   _____

   _____

   _____

Building Better Sentences

Correct and varied sentence structure is essential to the quality of your essay. For further practice with "An Alternative to University Education" go to Practice 5 on page 146 in Appendix 2.

WRITING THE INTRODUCTION

The introduction is the first part of an essay, usually the first paragraph. The introduction does not have to be written first, however. Some writers design and write this part last or at another point in their writing process.

From the basic outline that follows, you can see how the introduction fits into the essay. In this unit, you will learn about the introduction.

   I. Introduction (usually one paragraph)

  II. Body (one to four paragraphs)

 III. Conclusion (usually one paragraph)

There are many ways to write an introduction. Some writers begin with a question. Other writers give background information about the topic. The kind of introduction you choose depends on how you want to present the topic and the kind of essay you decide to write.

WHAT IS IN THE INTRODUCTION?

The introduction for most essays is one paragraph. This introductory paragraph usually consists of three parts:

INTRODUCTION = {
1. the hook
2. connecting information
3. the thesis statement (or writing plan).

Now look at each of these parts to see what they are and how they work in the introduction.

The Hook

The hook is the opening statement or statements. Just as a fisherman uses a hook to catch a fish, so a writer uses a hook to catch readers' attention. If a hook does its job well, readers will want to read the rest of the essay after they have read the hook. Writing a good hook is not easy. It requires a great deal of thought and practice.

There are many different ways to write a hook.

1. One common way to write a hook is to ask a question. If readers want to know the answer to the question, they are "hooked" and will read the essay. For example, a writer might begin an essay about the need for more government regulation of medicine with this question:

   How many people take medicine—even simple aspirin—every day?

   Most readers won't know the answer to this question, but they'll probably be hooked and want to find out more about the topic.

2. Another way to write a hook is to use an interesting observation. Here is an example:

> Asian economists are not sleeping well these days.

This observation makes readers want to know *why* economists are not sleeping well. This hook leads to the main idea of the essay, which will highlight the three main causes of recession in Asia.

Here's another example of an observation hook full of interesting details that leads readers to the subject of international trade:

> The average American is proud to be American and he is eager to talk about American products. However, the average American drives a Japanese or German car to work every morning. He wears cotton shirts made in Honduras and pants made in Bangladesh. His dinner salad has tomatoes from Mexico and salad dressing from France. Before he goes to bed, he will watch his favorite program on a Japanese television set.

3. Writers often begin an essay with a unique scenario to catch readers' attention:

> Traveling at more than one hundred miles an hour, he feels as though he is not moving. He is engulfed in complete silence. For a moment, it is as if he has entered another dimension.

Are you hooked? Do you want to read the rest of the essay? This essay is about the exciting sport of skydiving.

4. Sometimes writers use a famous quote as a hook, as in this example:

> "To be or not to be; that is the question."

Many readers may think that this hook will lead into a discussion of Shakespeare or the story of *Hamlet*. In fact, this hook begins an essay on the topic of suicide.

5. Some writers choose to use a statistic, especially one that is surprising or shocking, as a hook. Here are two examples:

> Over 20,000 people in the United States are killed in alcohol-related traffic accidents every year.

> If world temperatures continue to rise, Singapore and New York may be under water by the year 2050.

**On the Web
Try Unit 1
Activity 2**

WRITER'S NOTE: Hook versus Main Idea

In English writing, the main idea, or thesis, of an essay is usually in the introduction, but it's not often the first sentence. (The hook is usually the first sentence or the first few sentences.) If you begin an essay with a sentence stating the main idea, such as

> This essay will talk about the most embarrassing day of my life.

> or

> There are three ways to curb teen pregnancy.

your readers may not be interested in reading the rest of your essay. These sentences do not grab your readers' attention. Be sure to write a hook and put it first.

Connecting Information

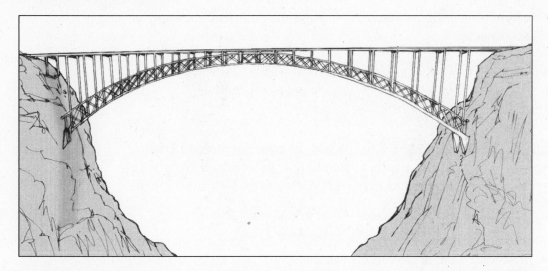

After the hook, the writer usually writes three to five sentences that help connect the reader and the topic. These sentences can be background information about the topic or they can be examples. The following sentences from Essay 1 on page 3 give examples of how Cinderella probably spent her days before she met the prince:

> Her daily routine was not glamorous. She did everything from sweeping the floors to cooking the meals. If someone had asked Cinderella, "Are there any household chores that you particularly hate?" she probably would have answered, "Why, none, of course. Housework is my duty!"

From these sentences, the reader has a good idea of what the topic might be: unpleasant household chores.

On the Web
Try Unit 1
Activity 3

WRITER'S NOTE: What Does the Reader Know?

A good writer does not jump into a topic too quickly. First, a good writer tries to imagine what the reader already knows about the topic. Then the writer can focus on bridging the gap between what the reader knows and what he or she needs to know about the topic. It is very important to keep the reader (the audience) in mind when writing academic essays.

The Thesis Statement

The thesis statement, or writing plan, is usually the last part of the introduction. It can be one or two sentences long. In the thesis statement, the writer tells the reader what to expect in the essay. Basically, there are two kinds of thesis statements, stated and implied. (These may also be called direct and indirect thesis statements.)

Stated Thesis Statement   Some writers want to give a specific outline of the paper in their thesis statement. For example:

> The main problems facing South American countries are a lack of job
> opportunities for citizens, increasing demand for better health care,
> and limited university programs for poor students.

From this statement, the reader knows that the body of the essay has three main parts. One part will discuss job opportunities, another part will talk about health care needs, and the last part will talk about university programs for poor students. This kind of thesis statement is called a *stated thesis*.

Implied Thesis Statement   Other writers are not so direct. On a similar topic as the previous example, these writers might use this statement:

> The important problems facing South American countries today
> require immediate attention.

From this statement, the reader expects to find a discussion of problems in South America. The reader is not given the specific information that will follow in the essay, but the general topic is clear. In this case, the reader must read on to find the supporting ideas of the argument. This kind of thesis statement is called an *implied thesis*.

Both stated and implied thesis statements are acceptable. It is up to the writer or the instructor to decide which approach to take.

On the Web
Try Unit 1
Activity 4

PRACTICE WITH HOOKS AND THESIS STATEMENTS

The following activities will give you practice writing hooks. You will also compare your hooks with those your classmates wrote. This will help you improve your understanding of how hooks work in essay introductions. Be prepared to explain why you think your hook will attract readers' attention and make them want to read the essay. You will also practice writing and identifying thesis statements.

Activity 6   **Practice with Hooks**

Essay 6

In this argumentative essay, the writer argues that mandatory retirement should be abolished.

1. The essay begins with the second sentence. Read the whole essay. Then write three possible hooks on the lines.

No More Mandatory Retirement

EXAMPLE ESSAY

|

Hook 1: _____

_____

Hook 2: _____

_____

Hook 3: _____

_____

Traditionally, people retire from their jobs when they reach the age of sixty-five. In some jobs, this is not an option but a requirement. Mandatory retirement for capable workers is wrong because it violates personal choice, discriminates against senior citizens, and wastes valuable skills as well as money.

2   One reason that mandatory retirement is wrong is that it takes away an individual's personal choice of continuing to work or retiring. The older working person should have the right to choose his or her retirement age. A person's right to life, liberty, and the pursuit of happiness (as written in the Declaration of Independence) is a very special thing. Forced retirement takes away people's livelihood, deprives them of their freedom to choose their line of work, and prevents them from pursuing happiness.

3   Second, mandatory retirement is surely a form of age discrimination. A young person might wonder why an older worker should be kept on the payroll when the company could hire someone who is younger and more creative. However, a younger person will not necessarily be a better or more creative worker. Age does not indicate the quality of a person's work. Many well-known artists, politicians, and writers developed their best works after the age of sixty. The common belief that a person's mind slows down after a certain age is nothing but a misconception.

4   In addition to the previous two points, there is the issue of quality of work. Older employees have knowledge and experience that can truly be beneficial. Unfortunately, many employers disregard this fact. Captain Al Haynes, age fifty-eight, was able to land a DC-10 that was out of control so that 186 of the 296 people aboard survived when it crashed. MacDonnell-Douglas, the maker of the DC-10, simulated the same problem forty-five times and not one time did they have a successful landing. Safety experts agree that the high survival rate among the passengers on the flight was due to Captain Haynes's aviation skills. It is doubtful that a less experienced pilot could have accomplished this feat. However, a year later, Captain Haynes had to retire because he had reached the age of sixty, the mandatory retirement age for pilots in the United States.

5   Many people, especially fresh college graduates, do not agree that retirement should be an option. They are worried that if older workers are allowed to continue in their jobs, there will not be enough openings for younger people. However, is there really a danger that older people will take away job opportunities from younger people? This is unlikely because younger workers and older workers rarely compete for the same jobs. In fact, older workers rarely seek entry-level positions. This type of faulty logic was used in the 1960s to oppose the passage of the civil rights laws that now protect women and minorities from employment discrimination. More importantly, the U.S. Department of Labor is concerned that labor shortages might occur when "baby boomers" retire after the year 2000. Therefore, employers should start looking for ways to attract experienced workers, not retire them.

6   In conclusion, the age of retirement should be decided by an individual's economic need, health status, and work preference. Our lives are our own, and we should be allowed to live our lives to the fullest potential. Without a doubt, mandatory retirement goes against fulfilling this potential and should not be a part of modern society.

2. In pairs or small groups, share the three hooks that you wrote with your classmates. Are any of them similar? Explain why you think your hooks will grab readers' attention.

Activity 7   **Thesis Statement Questions**

Answer these questions about the thesis statement in "No More Mandatory Retirement"

1. What is the thesis statement in the essay?

   _____

   _____

2. Is this a stated or implied thesis statement? _____

   Give the reason for your answer. _____

   _____

3. Rewrite the thesis statement as an implied thesis.

   _____

   _____

Building Better Sentences

Correct and varied sentence structure is essential to the quality of your essay. For further practice with "No More Mandatory Retirement," go to Practice 6 on page 147 in Appendix 2.

Activity 8   **More Practice with Hooks**

Essay 7

This comparison essay compares two different types of jobs.

1. The essay begins with the second sentence. Read the whole essay. Then write three possible hooks on the lines.

The Truth about Coaches and Business Managers

1

Hook 1: _____

_____

Hook 2: _____

_____

Hook 3: _____

_____

Coaches work outdoors while business managers stay in offices. Coaches train athletes'
bodies, but managers are more focused on detail-oriented matters. These differences,
however, pale in comparison to the similarities shared by the two professions, for the
main functions of athletic team coaches and business managers are very closely related.

2   One of the most fundamental similarities between athletic team coaches and business
managers is the task of leading the team members or employees. Coaches are responsible
for training their athletes and focusing on each individual's strengths and weaknesses.
Coaches also give directions to their players to improve their performance and commonly
give feedback after a game. Similarly, business managers are responsible for the proper
training of their employees. Managers use their people skills to ensure that each worker
is put in the job that suits his or her abilities best. In addition, managers typically give
periodic reviews of their employees as feedback on their job performance.

3   Another important similarity between the two professions is the ability to solve
problems between teammates or employees. Athletes tend to be very competitive, and
often this competitiveness leads to arguments in practice and during games. Coaches
know that this behavior is not productive in leading the team to victory, so they often act
as intermediaries. They listen to both sides and usually come up with words of wisdom
or advice to straighten out the problem. In the same way, a manager is often asked to
trouble-shoot for two or more employees who might not be getting along in the office.
Managers know that teamwork is vital to productivity, so they are trained to make sure
that the workplace runs smoothly.

4   Finally, both coaches and managers must represent their subordinates to the members
of higher management. Many social groups function as hierarchies, and the locker room
and office are no different. Coaches are regularly asked to report to the team owners with
updates on the season. They write up reports to keep the owners informed about who is

EXAMPLE ESSAY

EXAMPLE ESSAY

doing well, who is injured, and who is not performing up to par. In addition, they serve as the players' spokespersons. If players have a particular problem related to something other than their athletic performance, it is usually the coaches who end up speaking with the owners on the players' behalf. Like coaches, business managers are the links between the CEOs and lower-level employees. The business managers are given the tasks of overseeing employees and serving as go-betweens. Top management wants to remain aware of what is happening in the company, but they usually do not have the time to deal with such details. Business managers, therefore, serve as spokespeople to both ends of the hierarchy.

5   On the surface, the two occupations seem completely unrelated. The coach works outdoors and handles the pressures of physical exercise and strategies while the business manager works in a formal environment surrounded by modern technology. Upon further inspection, however, the job description of these two occupations is very closely related. Both careers are fundamental in improving communication and understanding of others.

2. In pairs or small groups, share the three hooks that you wrote with your classmates. Are any of them similar? Explain why you think your hooks will attract readers' attention.

Activity 9	Thesis Statement Questions

Answer these questions about the thesis statement in "The Truth about Coaches and Business Managers".

1. What is the thesis statement in the essay?

2. Is this a stated or implied thesis?
   Give the reason for your answer. _____

3. Rewrite the thesis statement as a stated thesis.

Building Better Sentences

Correct and varied sentence structure is essential to the quality of your essay. For further practice with "The Truth about Coaches and Business Managers," go to Practice 7 on page 148 in Appendix 2.

WRITING THE BODY

The body of an essay is the main part. It usually consists of three or four paragraphs between the introduction and the conclusion. The body follows a plan of organization that the writer usually determines before he or she starts writing. This organization varies depending on the kind of essay you are writing.

You can write the organizational plan of your essay in an outline. There are different levels of outlining. A **general outline** includes the main points, while a **specific,** or **detailed, outline** includes notes on even the smallest pieces of information. It is much easier to write an essay from a specific outline than from a general outline. However, most writers start with a general outline first and then add details.

WRITER'S NOTE: Using an Outline

The best essays have well-planned outlines that are carefully prepared before the writer starts writing.

Here is a **general outline** and a **specific outline** for Essay 7, "The Truth about Coaches and Business Managers," pages 27–29. Read and compare the two outlines.

General Outline	Specific Outline
I. Introduction	I. Introduction
A. Hook: pose a question	A. Hook: Are athletic coaches similar to business managers?
B. Connecting information	B. Connecting information:
	1. They work in different places and
	2. focus on different jobs.
C. Thesis: Similarities in coaches' and managers' jobs	C. Thesis: The two professions share many similarities, for the main functions of athletic team coaches and business managers are very closely related.
II. Body	II. Body
A. Similarity #1: Leading the employees	A. Similarity #1: Leading the employees
	1. Coaches train athletes
	a. focus on strengths
	b. focus on weaknesses
	c. give feedback

2. Managers train employees

    a. put employees in jobs that fit them best

    b. perform job reviews

B. Similarity #2: Solving Problems

B. Similarity #2: Solving Problems

    1. Coaches listen to athletes

        a. stop fights

        b. act as go-betweens

    2. Managers trouble-shoot in office

        a. importance of teamwork with employees

        b. try to get office mates to cooperate

C. Similarity #3: Representing the employees

C. Similarity #3: Representing the employees

    1. Coaches and owners

        a. give updates to owners

        b. discuss athletes' problems

    2. Managers and CEOs

        a. maintain control on behalf of the bosses

        b. update the CEOs on employee issues

III. Conclusion
Focus on maintaining communication

III. Conclusion: Both careers are fundamental in improving communication and understanding of others.

PRACTICE WITH OUTLINING AN ESSAY

General Outline

Activity 10   Making a General Outline

Here is a general outline for Essay 2, "How Do You Say . . . ?," on page 7. Read the essay again and complete this outline.

Title: _____

I. Introduction (paragraph 1)

    A. Hook: Ask a general question

    B. Connecting information

    C. Thesis statement: _____

    _____

II. Body

    A. Paragraph 2 topic sentence: _____

    _____

    B. Paragraph 3 topic sentence: _____

    _____

    C. Paragraph 4 topic sentence: _____

    _____

    D. Paragraph 5 topic sentence: _____

    _____

    E. Paragraph 6 topic sentence: _At first I was puzzled, but suddenly it all made sense._

III. Conclusion (paragraph 7)

    A. End of action

    B. Restatement of thesis

Specific Outline

Activity 11   **Making a Specific Outline**

Here is a specific outline for Essay 1, "Cinderella and Her Odious Household Chores," on pages 3–4. Read the essay again and complete this outline. You may use complete sentences if you wish, but be sure to include all of the specific information.

Title: "Cinderella and Her Odious Household Chores" _____

I. Introduction (paragraph 1)

   A. Hook: _____

   _____

   B. Connecting information: _____

   _____

   _____

   C. Thesis statement: _____

   _____

II. Body

   A. Paragraph 2

      1. Topic sentence (chore #1): _____

      _____

      2. Supporting ideas

         a. Attention to detail

            (1) Smoothing out the fabric

            (2) Following the seams

            (3) _____

            (4) _____

         b. Problem: _____

         _____

   B. Paragraph 3

      1. Topic sentence: (chore #2) _____

      _____

2. Supporting ideas

    a. Why we can't depend on dishwashers

    b. Negative aspects of this chore

      (1) Elbow grease

      (2) _____

      (3) _____

C. Paragraph 4

  1. Topic sentence (chore #3): _____

_____

  2. Supporting ideas

    a. Tasks

      (1) _____

      (2) Cleaning the sink

      (3) Cleaning the toilet

    b. Negative aspects

      (1) Bathroom is full of germs

      (2) _____

    c. Positive aspect: _____

III. Conclusion (paragraph 5)

  A. Maintaining a house includes chores.

  B. Take pride in doing a good job and getting through the three odious chores.

WRITER'S NOTE: Outline Length

    If your outline is too long, combine some of the ideas or eliminate ideas that don't add interest to the essay.

WRITING THE CONCLUSION

Some people think that writing the conclusion is the hardest part of writing an essay. For others, writing the conclusion is easy. When you write a conclusion, follow these guidelines:

1. Let the reader know that this is the conclusion. You can mark the conclusion with some kind of transition or connector that tells the reader that this is the final paragraph of the essay. (See Appendix 5 for a list of connectors.) Here are some examples:

   In conclusion,   From the information given,   To summarize,

   Sometimes the first sentence of the conclusion restates the thesis or main idea of the essay.

   This essay has presented three of the numerous problems that new parents face today.

2. Do not introduce new information in the conclusion. The conclusion should help the reader to reconsider the main ideas that you have given in the essay. Any new information in the concluding paragraph will sound like a continuation of the body of the essay.

3. Many writers find the conclusion difficult to write. It requires a great deal of thought and creativity, just as writing a good hook or thesis statement does. The kind of essay you are writing may determine the way you end the essay; however, two ideas can be helpful for any essay.

   a. The final sentence or sentences of an essay often give a *suggestion*, an *opinion*, or a *prediction* about the topic of the essay.

      - **Suggestion:**

        The facts strongly support the existence of a greenhouse warming effect on our atmosphere. It is vital, therefore, that we heed the warnings and do our best to keep this problem from getting worse.

      - **Opinion:**

        Certainly there are advantages and disadvantages to both of the plans presented here. However, because the second plan has more mass appeal than the former one, it would be a much better choice for the citizens of our country.

      - **Prediction:**

        This essay has presented strong arguments in favor of government control of television. Without this control, there will continue to be a decline in the moral values of American society.

   b. Sometimes the final sentence or sentences simply say that the issue has been discussed in the essay with so many strong, persuasive facts that the answer to the issue is now clear.

Once aware of this information, any reader would have to agree that animal testing is cruel and unethical and should be abolished.

After careful consideration of all the facts, readers will surely agree that the use of corporal punishment in our schools should be prohibited immediately.

On the Web
Try Unit 1
Activity 5

WRITER'S NOTE: Check the First and Last Paragraphs

After you write your essay, read the introductory paragraph and the concluding paragraph. These two paragraphs should contain much of the same information without sounding exactly the same.

On the Web
Try Unit 1
Activity 6

TOPICS FOR WRITING

Activity 12   **Essay Writing Practice**

Write an essay on one of the following suggested topics. Depending on the topic that you choose, you may need to do some research. Before you write, be sure to refer to the seven steps in the writing process in Appendix 1.

1. Write an essay about an important event that changed your life, such as marriage, the birth of a child, moving to a foreign country, or the loss of someone close to you.

2. Describe a festival or celebration in your culture. Discuss the history of the event, its meaning, and how it is celebrated.

3. Many inventions of the twentieth century, such as television and the microwave oven, have changed our lives. Write an essay in which you discuss the effects of one invention on society.

4. Some people say that people are born with their intelligence and outside factors do not affect intelligence very much. They believe that nature (what we are born with) is more important than nurture (environment). Other people say that intelligence is mostly the result of the interaction between people and their environment. These people believe that nurture is more important than nature. Write an essay in which you defend one of these points of view.

5. Write about a movie that you saw on television or at the cinema. Summarize the story and tell what you liked and did not like about it.

Narrative Essays

GOAL: To learn how to write a narrative essay

LANGUAGE FOCUS: Connectors and time relationship words

WHAT IS A NARRATIVE ESSAY?

A narrative essay tells a story. Telling stories has always been an important part of human history. An essay that tells a story is called a *narrative* essay. Another word for *story* is *narrative*. Even though the narrative essay has the same basic form as most other academic essays, it allows the writer to be more creative than academic essays usually do.

Several important elements make up a story.

Setting	The setting is the location where the action in a story happens.
Theme	The theme is the basic idea of the story. Very often the theme will deal with a topic that is common in life or human nature, such as greed, envy, love, independence, and so on.
Mood	The mood is the feeling or atmosphere that the writer creates for the story. It could be happy, hopeful, suspenseful, scary. Both the setting and descriptive vocabulary create the mood in a narrative.
Characters	The characters are the people in the story. They are affected by the mood, and they react to the events in which they are involved.
Plot	The plot is what happens in the story, that is, the sequence of events. The plot often includes a climax or turning point at which the characters or events change.

On the Web
Try Unit 2
Activity 1

THE INTRODUCTION

The introduction is the paragraph that begins your story. This is where you describe the setting, introduce the characters, and prepare the reader for the action to come. Of course, the introduction should have a hook and a thesis.

The Narrative Hook

You learned in Unit 1 that the hook in an essay is the part of the introduction—usually the first sentence or two—that grabs readers' attention. Hooks are especially important in narrative essays because they help "set the stage" for the story. The hook makes readers start guessing about what will happen next. Let's look at the hook from the essay in Activity 1.

> I had never been more anxious in my life. I had just spent the last three
> endless hours trying to get to the airport so that I could travel home.

Does this hook make you want to know what happened to the narrator? The hook should make the reader ask *wh-* questions about the essay. You may have thought of questions like these when you read the preceding example sentences:

> *Who* is the narrator and why is he or she anxious?
> *Where* is the airport?
> *What* made the trip to the airport seem endless?
> *Why* is this person going home?

Activity 1 — Identifying Hooks

Read the sentences. Which three of these sentences are NOT good hooks for narrative essays? Put an X next to these sentences. Be ready to explain why you think these sentences do not work well as hooks for narrative essays.

1. _____ The roar of racecar engines ripped through the blazing heat of the day.

2. _____ It was freezing on that sad December day.

3. _____ After my brother's accident, I sat alone in the hospital waiting room.

4. _____ My friend and I shouldn't have been walking home alone so late on that dark winter night.

5. _____ Whales are by far the largest marine mammals.

6. _____ She gave her friend a birthday gift.

7. _____ The gleaming snow lay over the treacherous mountain like a soft white blanket, making the terrain seem safe instead of deadly.

8. _____ The Russian dictionary that we use in our language class has 500 pages.

9. _____ Sandra never expected to hear the deadly sound of a rattlesnake in her kitchen garden.

**On the Web
Try Unit 2
Activity 2**

10. _____ A shot rang out in the silence of the night.

The Thesis

Usually the thesis states the main idea of the essay and tells what the organization of the information will be. However, in a narrative essay, the thesis introduces the action that begins in the first paragraph of the essay. Look at these example thesis statements:

> Now, as I watched the bus driver set my luggage on the airport sidewalk, I realized that my frustration had only just begun.

> I wanted my mother to watch me race down the steep hill, so I called out her name and then nudged my bike forward.

> Because his pride wouldn't allow him to apologize, Ken now had to fight the bully, and he was pretty sure that he wouldn't win.

The example sentences do not tell the reader what happens. They only introduce the action that will follow. The paragraphs in the body will develop the story.

THE BODY

The body of your narrative essay contains most of the plot—the supporting information. The action in the plot can be organized in many different ways. One way is **chronological,** or time, order. In this method each paragraph gives more information about the story as it proceeds in time: the first paragraph usually describes the first event, the second paragraph describes the second event, and so on.

Transitional Sentences

In a chronological organization, each paragraph ends with a **transitional sentence.** Transitional sentences have two purposes: (1) to signal the end of action in one paragraph, and (2) to provide a link to the action of the next paragraph. These sentences are vital because they give your story unity and allow the reader to follow the action easily. The following example is from Essay 8 on page 42, paragraphs 2 and 3. Notice how the ideas in the last sentence of paragraph 2 (the transitional sentence, underlined) and the first sentence of paragraph 3 (italicized) are connected.

EXAMPLE ESSAY

2 This was my first visit to the international section of the airport, and nothing was familiar. I could not make sense of the signs. Where was the ticket counter? Where should I take my luggage? I had no idea where the customs line was. I began to panic. What time was it? Where was my airplane? <u>I had to find help because I could not be late</u>!
3 *I tried to ask a passing businessman for help, but all my words came out wrong.* He just scowled and walked away. What had happened? I had been in this country for a whole semester, and I could not even remember how to ask for directions. This was awful! Another bus arrived at the terminal, and the passengers came out carrying all sorts of luggage. Here was my chance! I could follow them to the right place, and I would not have to say a word to them.

WRITER'S NOTE: Storytelling Tip

If you describe the sights, smells, and sounds of the story, you will bring the story alive for the reader.

THE CONCLUSION

Like academic essays, narrative essays need to have concluding ideas. In the **concluding paragraph,** you finish describing the action in the essay. The final sentence can have two functions:

1. It can deliver the moral for the story, or tell the reader what the character(s) learned from the experience.

2. It can make a prediction or a revelation (disclosure of something that was not known before) about future actions that will happen as a result of the events in the story.

Look at these examples:

Moral: The little boy had finally learned that telling the truth was the most important thing to do.

Prediction/ Revelation: I can only hope that one day I will be able to do the same for another traveler who is suffering through a terrible journey.

Every Christmas Eve, my wife and I return to that magical spot and remember the selfless act that saved our lives.

WRITER'S NOTE: Effective Narrative Essays

These are a few of the elements in an effective narrative essay:

- a thesis that sets up the action in the introduction
- transition sentences that connect events and help the reader follow the story
- a conclusion that ends the story action and provides a moral or revelation

EXAMPLE NARRATIVE ESSAY

A good way to learn what a narrative looks like is to read and study an example.

Activity 2 **Studying an Example Essay**

Read and study this narrative essay. Answer the questions. These questions will help you understand the content and the organization of the essay. As you read, look at the final sentence in paragraphs 2, 3, 4, and 5. Does each one prepare you for the action to come?

Essay 8

In this narrative essay, a traveler has a frustrating experience at the airport.

1. Have you ever had trouble trying to get to someplace very important? Where were you going? Why were you having problems?

2. What is a hero? What do you consider to be a heroic act?

<u>Frustration</u> at the Airport

1   I had never been more anxious in my life. I had just spent the last three endless hours trying to get to the airport so that I could travel home. Now, as I watched the bus driver set my luggage on the airport sidewalk, I realized that my frustration had only just begun.

2   This was my first visit to the international section of the airport, and nothing was familiar. I could not make sense of all the signs. Where was the ticket counter? Where should I take my luggage? I had no idea where the customs line was. I began to panic. What time was it? Where was my airplane? I had to find help because I could not be late!

3   I tried to ask a passing businessman for help, but all my words came out wrong. He just <u>scowled</u> and walked away. What had happened? I had been in this country for a whole semester, and I could not even remember how to ask for directions. This was awful! Another bus arrived at the <u>terminal</u>, and the passengers came out carrying all sorts of luggage. Here was my chance! I could follow them to the right place, and I would not have to say a word to them.

4   I dragged my enormous suitcase behind me and followed the group. We finally got to the elevators. Oh, no!! They all fit in, but there was not enough room for me. I watched in <u>despair</u> as the elevator doors closed. I had no idea what to do next. I got on the elevator when it returned and <u>gazed</u> at all the buttons. Which one would it be? I pressed button 3. The elevator slowly climbed up to the third floor and <u>jerked</u> to a stop. A high squeaking noise announced the opening of the doors, and I looked around <u>timidly</u>.

5   Tears formed in my eyes as I saw the deserted lobby and realized that I would miss my airplane. Just then an old airport employee <u>shuffled</u> around the corner. He saw that I was lost and asked if he could help. He gave me his handkerchief to dry my eyes as I related my <u>predicament</u>. He smiled kindly, took me by the hand, and led me down a long hallway. We walked up some stairs, turned a corner, and at last, there was customs! He led me past all the lines of people and pushed my luggage to the inspection counter.

6   When I turned to thank him for all his help, he was gone. I will never know that wonderful man's name, but I will always remember his unexpected <u>courtesy</u>. He helped me when I needed it the most. I can only hope that one day I will be able to do the same for another traveler who is suffering through a terrible journey.

frustration: feeling of impatience and discouragement

scowl: to frown

terminal: an arrival and departure point for some forms of mass transportation

despair: the condition of having no hope

gaze: to look at slowly and steadily

jerk: to move with an abrupt motion

timidly: hesitantly or fearfully

shuffle: to walk by sliding one's feet along the ground

predicament: a troubling situation

courtesy: a kind or polite action

WRITER'S NOTE: Verb Tense in Narrative Essays

Most narrative essays are written in the simple past tense because narratives usually tell events that have already happened.

3. What is the narrative hook?

_____

_____

4. Do you think the hook is effective (did it grab your attention)? Why, or why not?

_____

_____

5. Where is the setting of this story (where does it take place)?

_____

6. What is the theme, or the basic idea, of "Frustration at the Airport"?

_____

_____

7. What do you think the mood of the story is? What feeling or atmosphere does the writer create?

_____

_____

8. Who are the characters?

_____

_____

9. What verb tense is used in "Frustration at the Airport"? _____ Write any five verbs here.

_____

_____

10. Is the story arranged in chronological, or time, order? In a few words, describe what happens first, second, third, and so on.

_____

_____

_____

11. Underline the transitional sentences.

12. Does the story end with a moral or a revelation? If so, write it here:

_____

_____

Building Better Sentences

Correct and varied sentence structure is essential to the quality of your essay. For further practice with "Frustration at the Airport," go to Practice 8 on page 149 in Appendix 2.

Activity 3   **Outlining Practice**

Below is an outline for "Frustration at the Airport." Some of the information is missing. Reread the essay beginning on page 41 and complete the outline.

Title: _____

I. Introduction (paragraph 1)

    A. Hook: I had never been so anxious in my life! _____

    B. Connecting information _____

C. Thesis statement: _____

_____

II. Body

A. Paragraph 2 (event 1) topic sentence:

This was my first visit to the international section of the airport, and nothing was familiar.

SUPPORT

1. The signs were confusing.

2. I began to panic.

3. Transition sentence:

_____

B. Paragraph 3 (event 2) topic sentence:

_____

SUPPORT

1. He scowled and walked away.

2. I couldn't remember how to ask for directions.

3. _____

4. Transition sentence:

_____

C. Paragraph 4 (event 3) topic sentence:

I dragged my enormous suitcase behind me and followed the group.

SUPPORT

1. _____

2. I got on the elevator and looked at the buttons.

3. _____

4. Transition sentence:

_____

D. Paragraph 5 (event 4) topic sentence:

<u>Tears formed in my eyes as I saw the deserted lobby and realized that I would miss my airplane.</u>

1. An airport employee offered to help.

2. _____

3. _____

3. Transition sentence: <u>He led me past all the lines of people and pushed my luggage to</u>

<u>the inspection counter.</u>

III. Conclusion (paragraph 6)

A. Close of the action:

_____

B. <u>I will never know his name, but I will always remember his unexpected courtesy.</u>

C. _____

D. Final sentence (prediction or revelation):

_____

Activity 4   Adding Supporting Information

The following narrative essay is missing large parts of the story (supporting information in the body). As you read, add information that moves the story along. Be sure to write transition sentences at the end of paragraphs 2, 3, and 4. If you need more space, use a separate piece of paper. Be as creative as you like!

Essay 9

Making Your Own Luck

1   I should never have thrown the chain letter away. The letter warned me that if I did, I would have one day of bad luck. I did not believe it, so I threw the silly thing in the garbage. I thought the friend who sent me the letter was just a superstitious fool. Letters do not bring you luck. You make your own! That night, however, as I feel asleep, I had the uncomfortable feeling that something was not quite right.

2   When I woke up the next morning, I was surprised to find that I had overslept and would be late for work. As I rushed down the stairs to eat a quick breakfast, I tripped over my cat and

_____

_____

_____

_____

3   On my way to work, I decided to take a shortcut through an old part of town. _____

_____

_____

_____

4   When I arrived at work, I found a note on my desk from my boss. She wanted to see me right away. I took a deep breath and walked into her office. As I stepped inside, I noticed a scowl on her face.

_____

_____

_____

_____

5   Finally, after a long and difficult day, I returned home to find that my air conditioner was broken. I could not take it anymore! It had been the worst day of my life, and I did not want anything else to happen. I rushed to the garbage can and dug around for the chain letter I had thrown away the day before. It was covered with coffee grounds and potato peels, but I could still read the words: "Send ten copies of this letter to your friends and you will have good luck for a year." I sat down at the kitchen table and began to make copies for ten of my friends. They could take their chances, but I was not going to have any more bad luck!

Brazil covers almost half of the South American continent. Few Brazilians can say that they have traveled <u>extensively</u> within its borders. Because of Brazil's large size, its weather varies greatly from one area to another. Like Brazil, the United States takes up a significant portion of its continent (North America), so most Americans have visited only a few of the fifty states. In addition, the United States has a wide range of <u>climates</u>. While the Northeast is experiencing snowstorms, cities like Miami, Florida, can have temperatures over 85 degrees Fahrenheit.

3   Another similarity between Brazil and the United States is the diversity of ethnic groups. Brazil was colonized by Europeans, and its culture has been greatly influenced by this fact. However, the identity of the Brazilian people is not <u>solely</u> a product of Western civilization. Brazil is a "melting pot" of many ethnic groups that immigrated there and mixed with the native people. The United States also has a diversity of ethnic groups representing the early colonists from northern Europe as well as groups from Africa, the Mediterranean, Asia, and South America. The mixture of cultures and customs has worked to form ethnically rich cultures in both countries.

4   Finally, <u>individualism</u> is an important value for both Brazilians and Americans. Brazil works hard to defend the <u>concept</u> of freedom of choice. Citizens believe that they have the right to do and be whatever they desire as long as they don't hurt others. Individualism and freedom of choice also exist in the United States, where freedom is perhaps the highest value of the people. Some may believe that the desire for individual expression is divisive and can make a country weak. However, the ability of people to be whatever they want makes both countries strong.

5   Although Brazil and the United States are unique countries, there are remarkable similarities in their size, ethnic groups, and personal values. Some people tend to believe that their culture and country are without equal. Nevertheless, it is important to remember that people as a whole have more in common than they generally think they do.

hemisphere: one half of the world

extensively: widely; over a large area

climate: the usual weather of a region
   over a period of time

solely: only; entirely

individualism: the belief that each person
   works for his or her own goals

concept: idea

3. What subjects does the writer compare in this essay?

    _____

4. What method of organization does the writer use, point-by-point or block?

    _____

5. What is the hook for this essay? Write it here.

    _____

6. Underline the thesis statement. Is the thesis restated in the conclusion (paragraph 5)? If yes, underline that sentence in the conclusion.

7. Supporting sentences: In paragraph 2, the author writes about the ways in which size affects Brazil and the United States. List that information here.

The Effects of Size	
Brazil	**United States**
1. _____	1. _____
_____	_____
2. _____	2. _____
_____	_____
3. _____	3. _____
_____	_____

8. Reread the concluding paragraph of "Not As Different As You Think." Does the writer offer **a suggestion, an opinion,** or **a prediction**? Circle the appropriate phrase in bold and write the sentence from the essay.

_____

_____

Building Better Sentences

Correct and varied sentence structure is essential to the quality of your essay. For further practice with "Not As different As You think," go to Practice 12 on page 153 in Appendix 2.

DEVELOPING COMPARISON ESSAYS

In this next section, you will develop comparison essays as you make an outline, write supporting information, study connectors, and choose a topic. In the following activities, you will practice the skills you need to write an effective comparison essay.

Activity 2   **Outlining Practice**

Below is a specific outline for "Not As Different As You Think." (For a review of specific outlines, see pages 64–65.) Some of the information is missing. Reread the essay beginning on page 66 and complete the outline.

Title: _____

   I. Introduction (paragraph 1)

      A. Hook: All countries in the world are unique. _____

      B. Connecting information: Different location, size, culture

      C. Thesis statement: _____

      _____

  II. Body

      A. Paragraph 2 (similarity 1) topic sentence:

      _____

SUPPORT

1. Brazil's characteristics

    a. Size: _____

    b. Travel: Few Brazilians have traveled extensively in their country.

    c. Climate: _____

2. _____

    a. _____

    b. Travel: _____

    c. Climate: The weather can be extremely different from the north to the south.

B. Paragraph 3 (similarity 2) topic sentence:

Another similarity is the diversity of ethnic groups.

SUPPORT

1. Brazil

    a. _____

    b. Other ethnic groups.

    c. _____

2. United States

    a. Europe

    b. Africa

    c. the Mediterranean

    d. _____

    e. _____

C. Paragraph 4 (similarity 3) topic sentence:

_____

SUPPORT

1. Brazilians' belief in freedom: _____

_____

2. _____

_____

III. Conclusion (paragraph 5)

A. Restated thesis: _____

_____

B. Opinion: Nevertheless, it is important to remember that people as a whole have more in common than they generally think they do.

WRITER'S NOTE: Ask Questions

How can you develop details and facts that will support your main ideas (topic sentences) in each paragraph? One of the best ways to write this supporting information is to ask yourself questions about the topic—*Where? Why? When? Who? What? How?*

Activity 3   **Supporting Information**

The following comparison essay is missing the supporting information. As you read the essay, work with a partner to write supporting sentences for each paragraph. If you need more space, use a separate piece of paper. After you finish, compare your supporting information with that of other students.

Note: This essay follows the point-by-point organizational pattern.

Essay 13

Many car buyers want to know the differences between foreign and domestic cars. In this essay, you and the writer provide some of that information.

Foreign or Domestic?

1 Transportation today is much different from the way it was fifty years ago. At that time, people who wanted to buy an automobile had a small variety to choose from. Nowadays, there are so many choices that it could take months to look at all the cars on the market. Often a buyer must first choose between a foreign car and a domestic car. To reach a decision, a buyer should compare foreign and domestic cars in terms of quality and dependability, maintenance, and style.

2 Foreign and domestic cars vary in quality and dependability. _____

_____

_____

_____

_____

_____

3 Another thing to consider is maintenance. _____

_____

_____

_____

_____

_____

_____

_____

EXAMPLE ESSAY

EXAMPLE ESSAY

4 Finally, there is the subject of style. _____

_____

_____

_____

_____

_____

5 All cars are used for transportation, but it is important to remember that there are differences in quality and dependability, service options, and style, depending on the make and model. Choosing between a domestic vehicle or an imported one is a personal decision. Careful consideration of the information presented here will make choosing a car less complicated.

Building Better Sentences

Correct and varied sentence structure is essential to the quality of your essay. For further practice with "Foreign or Domestic?" go to Practice 13 on page 154 in Appendix 2.

LANGUAGE FOCUS: Connectors for Comparison Essays

Writers use connectors in a well-organized essay to help clarify the main ideas. Connectors help readers by providing logical connections between sentences, ideas, and paragraphs. Notice that when these words (sometimes including the phrase that follows) begin sentences, they are followed by a comma.

The following two charts show connectors that can be used in comparison essays. Notice that the first chart is for comparison words and phrases and the second chart is for contrast words and phrases. (For a more complete list of connectors, see Appendix 5.)

Connectors That Show Comparison

Between sentences or paragraphs	Example
In addition,	Both Red Beauty and Midnight Dream roses are known for the size of their blooms, their color, and their fragrance. **In addition,** they are easy to grow.

Similarly,	The Midnight Dream rose won awards in local contests last year. **Similarly,** the Red Beauty Rose was singled out for its beauty.
Likewise,	The blooms of Red Beauty roses last longer than those of most other roses. **Likewise,** the blooms of the Midnight Dream rose are long-lasting.
Compared to . . . ,	**Compared to** many other roses, the blooms of Red Beauty and Midnight Dream roses last a long time.

Connectors That Show Contrast

Between sentences or paragraphs	Example
However, On the other hand,	**However, (On the other hand,)** some of their differences are not very obvious.
In contrast,	Red Beauty has a strong, sweet fragrance. **In contrast,** Midnight Dream's fragrance is light and fruity.
Although . . . ,	**Although** they both have red flowers, Midnight Dream roses are darker than Red Beauty roses.
Even though . . . ,	**Even though** they are both long-stemmed roses, Red Beauty stems are thin and covered with thorns while Midnight Dream stems are thick and have almost no thorns.
Unlike . . . ,	**Unlike** Red Beauty, Midnight Dream roses are relatively inexpensive.

WWW

**On the Web
Try Unit 3
Activity 2**

Activity 4   **Connectors**

Read the next student essay and circle the appropriate connector in parentheses. Refer to the list in the Language Focus, if necessary.

Essay 14

The writer in this essay compares the educational systems in Taiwan and the United States.

Education in the East and the West

1 Americans have often asked me why I came from Taiwan to study in the United States. They expect me to say something like "to learn English." (*However/Another*), to me, coming here to study involves more than just learning English. It involves an opportunity to experience a completely different educational system. Because I have studied in both countries, I have seen several areas in which education in Taiwan and education in the United States are different.

2 Students' expectations in the classroom in Taiwan are different from those in the United States. Generally speaking, Taiwanese students are quieter and participate less in class. They are not encouraged to express their ideas unless asked. They are taught that asking teachers a question is seen as a challenge to the teacher's authority. There is little emphasis on developing student creativity and thinking skills. Students are expected to memorize everything they are assigned. (*In addition/However*), in the United States the curriculum emphasizes individual thinking, group discussion, and self-expression. (*Unlike/Even though*) their Taiwanese counterparts, American students are encouraged to ask questions, express their own opinions, and think for themselves.

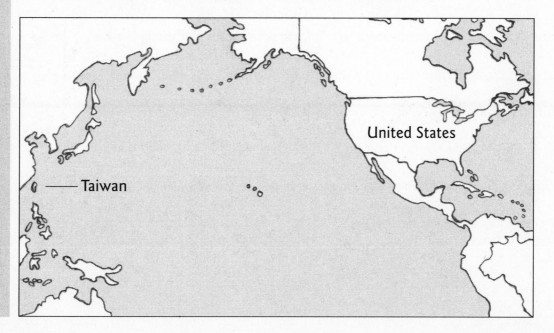

EXAMPLE ESSAY

3 (*However/In addition*), there is a great disparity in the educational goals of Taiwanese and American schools. After twelve years of compulsory education, Taiwanese students have to pass an entrance exam in order to get into a university. The higher students score on this test, the better the university they can enter. Taiwanese culture puts a strong emphasis on university admission because getting into the right university can guarantee future success. As a result, schools often "teach to the test" instead of providing more moral, social, and physical education. (*In contrast/Likewise*), the goals of the American educational system include teaching students how to learn and helping them reach their maximum potential. American teachers give their students the freedom to think and solve problems on their own; they do not merely prepare students to answer questions for an entrance exam.

4 The last obvious difference between the two countries' educational systems is the role of extracurricular activities such as sports programs and special interest clubs. (*Even though/Compared to*) every Taiwanese school claims that it pays equal attention to moral, intellectual, and physical education, the real focus is on passing the university admissions exam. Little emphasis is placed on activities outside of the classroom. Teachers can even borrow time from extracurricular activities to give students more practice in the areas where they have weaknesses. (*On the other hand/Likewise*), American educational institutions consider the development of social and interpersonal skills as important as the development of intellectual skills. It is believed that by participating in these outside activities, students can demonstrate their special talents, level of maturity, and leadership qualities.

5 Education is vital to everyone's future success. While it may take ten years to grow a tree, a sound educational system may take twice as long to take root. (*However/ Although*) Taiwan and the United States have different educational systems, both countries have the same ultimate goal: to educate their citizens as well as they can. This goal can be reached only if people take advantage of all the educational opportunities given to them. That is why I came to the United States to study, grow, and become a better person.

Building Better Sentences

Correct and varied sentence structure is essential to the quality of your essay. For further practice with "Education in the East and the West," go to Practice 14 on page 155 in Appendix 2.

IDEAS BRAINSTORMING

You will be asked to write comparison essays in many of your classes. Often, you will be given the two subjects to be compared, such as two works of literature, two kinds of chemical compounds, or two political beliefs. When you have to choose your own subjects for comparison, the following brainstorming tips will help you.

Tips for brainstorming subjects

1. The subjects should have something in common.

   Soccer and hockey are both fast-paced games that require a player to score a point by putting an object into a goal guarded by another player.

2. The two subjects must also have some differences.

   The most obvious differences between the two games are the playing field, the protective equipment, and the number of players.

3. You need to have enough information on each topic to make your comparisons.

   If you choose two sports that are not well-known, it might be more difficult to find information about them.

Make a list

A good way to determine whether you have enough information about similarities and differences between two subjects is to brainstorm a list. Read the information in the lists below.

Ice Hockey

played on ice

6 players on a team

uses a puck

(very popular sport)

(players use lots of protective pads)

(can't touch the puck with your hands)

(goal = puck in the net)

Soccer

played on a grass field

11 players on a team

uses a soccer ball

(very popular sport)

(players use some protective pads)

(can't touch the ball with your hands)

(goal = ball in the net)

As you can see, soccer and hockey have many similarities and a few differences. Notice that the similarities are circled. These are "links" between the two subjects. A writer could use these links to highlight the similarities between the two games or to lead into a discussion of the differences between them ("Although both soccer and hockey are popular, more schools have organized soccer teams than hockey . . . ").

Make a Venn diagram

Another way to brainstorm similarities and differences is to use a Venn diagram. (Perhaps you have used Venn diagrams in math class.) A Venn diagram is a visual representation of the similarities and differences between two concepts. Here is a Venn diagram of the characteristics of hockey and soccer.

HOCKEY		**SOCCER**
Played on ice	Very popular sport	Played on a grass field
6 players on a team	Can't touch puck/ball with hands	11 players on a team
Uses a puck		Uses a soccer ball
Uses lots of protective pads	Score = puck/ball in goal	Uses some protective pads

---

Activity 5 — Identifying Good Subjects

Below are pairs of potential subjects for a comparison essay. Write "yes" on the line under the pairs that would be good subjects and explain briefly what could be compared. Write "no" under the subjects that would not be good choices and change one or both of them into more suitable subjects. The first two have been done for you as examples.

1. living in houses / living in apartments

   Yes. Compare costs, privacy, space

2. international travel / 747 airplanes

   No. Change "747 airplanes" to "domestic travel"

3. high school / college

4. the weather in Toronto / tourist attractions in Toronto

_____

5. wild animals / animals in a zoo

_____

6. computers / computer keyboards

_____

7. hands / feet

_____

8. the surface of the ocean floor / the surface of the continents

_____

9. the Earth / the North American continent

_____

10. Chinese food / Mexican food

_____

On the Web
Try Unit 3
Activity 3

WRITER'S NOTE: Writing from Personal Experience

Many international students like to compare and contrast certain features of their cultures to those of other cultures. These topics usually lead to interesting essays that engage readers.

Activity 6   **Working with a Topic**

1. Choose one topic from the list or use your own idea for a topic. If you want to use an original idea, talk to your teacher to see if it is appropriate for a comparison essay.

two famous people   two sports   two movies

two places   two machines   two celebrations or holidays

two desserts   two kinds of education   two kinds of professions

2. Use the following chart to brainstorm a list of information about each subject.
   If you like, use the soccer/hockey list on page 78 as a guide.

TOPIC: _____

Subject 1   Subject 2

_____   _____

_____   _____

_____   _____

_____   _____

_____   _____

_____   _____

_____   _____

_____   _____

3. Now fill in the Venn diagram using the information from the preceding chart.

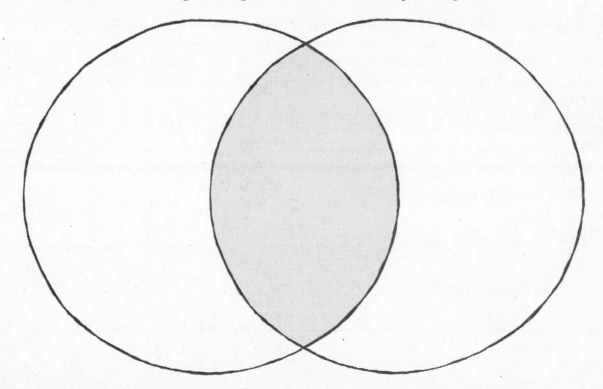

4. Decide if you are going to compare mainly the similarities or the differences or both between the two subjects in your comparison essay. Then choose three or four main points that you will use and list them here.

a. _____

b. _____

c. _____

d. _____

On the Web
Try Unit 3
Activity 4—6

WRITER'S NOTE: Ideas for Supporting Information

In the next activity, you will develop supporting information. Here are some ideas to help you get started. For a point of comparison,

- give a description.
- give examples.
- give a cause.
- give an effect.

Activity 7   Planning with an Outline

Now that you have a topic, it's time to create an outline for your comparison essay. Use the outline below as a guide to help you brainstorm a more detailed plan for your essay. For this activity, use the point-by-point method of organization (see pages 64–65). You may need to use either more or fewer points under each heading. Include your ideas from Activity 6. Write complete sentences where possible.

TOPIC: _____

I. Introduction (paragraph 1)

A. Hook: _____

B. Connecting information:

_____

C. Thesis statement: _____

_____

II. Body

A. Paragraph 2 (first point of comparison) topic sentence: _____

_____

SUPPORT

    1. _____

       a. _____

       b. _____

    2. _____

       a. _____

       b. _____

B. Paragraph 3 (second point of comparison) topic sentence: _____

_____

SUPPORT

    1. _____

       a. _____

       b. _____

    2. _____

       a. _____

       b. _____

C. Paragraph 4 (third point of comparison) topic sentence: _____

_____

SUPPORT

1. _____

   a. _____

   b. _____

2. _____

   a. _____

   b. _____

III. Conclusion (paragraph 5)

   A. Restated thesis: _____

   _____

   B. Suggestion, opinion, or prediction: _____

   _____

Activity 8   Peer Editing Your Outline

Exchange outlines with another student. Read each other's outlines and make comments using Peer Editing Sheet 3 on page 189.

Activity 9   Writing a Comparison Essay

After you have read your classmate's review of your outline, think about any changes you want to make in your essay. Make sure you have enough information to develop your supporting sentences. Then write your comparison essay. Save all your work, including your brainstorming pages or notes, revised drafts, and the Peer Editing Sheet. Be sure to refer to the seven steps in the writing process in Appendix 1 on page 131.

Activity 10 **Peer Editing Your Essay**

Exchange comparison essays from Activity 9 with a partner. Then use Peer Editing Sheet 4 on page 191 to help you comment on your partner's paper. It is important to offer positive comments that will help the writer.

TOPICS FOR WRITING

Activity 11 **Essay Writing Practice**

Here are more ideas for topics for a comparison essay. Before you write, be sure to refer to the seven steps in the writing process in Appendix 1.

1. Compare a book to its movie version, for example, *The Great Gatsby* by F. Scott Fitzgerald. How are the two alike and different? Are the characters and the plot the same? Do you like the movie or the book better, and why?

2. Compare the situation in a country before and after an important historical event, for example, Cuba before and after Fidel Castro came to power.

3. Discuss two kinds of music, such as classical and rock. A few points of comparison might be artists, instruments, audiences, and popularity.

4. Show how the world has changed since the invention of the airplane. How did people travel before its invention? How often did people travel? How far were they usually able to go and how long did it take to get there?

5. Show the similarities and differences in the ways that two cultures celebrate an important event such as a birthday, wedding, or funeral.

Cause-Effect Essays

GOAL: To learn how to write a cause-effect essay

LANGUAGE FOCUS: Connectors for cause-effect essays

WHAT IS A CAUSE-EFFECT ESSAY?

A cause-effect essay shows the reader the relationship between something that happens and its consequences, or between actions and results. For example, if too much commercial fishing is allowed in the North Atlantic Ocean (action), the fish population in some areas may diminish or disappear (result). Cause-effect essays can be informative and insightful.

You will study two kinds of cause-effect essays. Very simply, in one method, the writer focuses on the *causes* of something. This is called the **focus-on-causes** method. In the second method, the writer emphasizes the effects or *results* of a cause. This is called the **focus-on-effects** method.

Imagine that your teacher gives you the topic of culture shock to write about. You have the choice of writing either a cause essay or an effect essay.

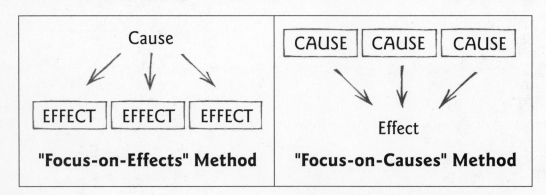

FOCUS-ON-CAUSES METHOD

If you decide to use the focus-on-causes method, you would focus mainly on the causes of culture shock—perhaps three or four things that lead people to suffer from culture shock. Each paragraph would address one of these ideas. You might begin with this question: **Why do people feel culture shock?**

FOCUS-ON-EFFECTS METHOD

On the other hand, you may want to emphasize the effects of culture shock—perhaps three or four things that people with culture shock feel or experience. By choosing the focus-on-effects method, your body paragraphs would explain how culture shock affects people. Each paragraph would address one idea. You might begin with this question: **What happens to people who experience culture shock?**

WRITER'S NOTE: Cause-Effect Essay Methods

Essays that use the focus-on-causes method answer the question "Why does something happen?"

Essays that use the focus-on-effects method answer the question "What happens when . . . ?"

On the Web
Try Unit 4
Activity 1

EXAMPLE CAUSE-EFFECT ESSAY

A good way to help you learn how to write a cause-effect essay is to study an example. The following example is a cause essay that answers the question "Why do people lie?"

| Activity I | Studying an Example Essay |

Read and study the following essay. Work with a partner to answer the questions before and after the essay. These questions will help you understand the content and the organization of the essay.

Essay 15

This essay may make you think twice before you tell another lie.

1. Why do you think people lie?

2. Is it ever acceptable to lie? Give examples of acceptable and unacceptable lies.

Why Do We Lie?

1   As little children, most of us were taught the virtue of honesty through fairy tales and other stories. The story of Pinocchio, who begins life as a <u>puppet</u>, teaches us the importance of telling the truth. The boy who lied by "crying wolf" too many times lost all his sheep as well as the trust of his fellow villagers. There is a story that young George Washington cut down a cherry tree. From this story, American children learn that Washington earns his father's praise only when he admits what he has done. Even though we know that "honesty is the best policy," why do we often lie in our everyday lives? The fact is that we lie for many reasons.

2   We sometimes lie to minimize our mistakes. While it is true that we all make <u>blunders</u> sometimes, some of us do not have the courage to admit them because we might be blamed for the errors. For example, students might lie to their teachers about unfinished homework. They might say that they left the work at home when, in fact, they did not even do the work. These students do not want to seem irresponsible, so they make up an excuse—a lie—to save face.

3   Another reason we lie is to get out of situations that we do not want to be in or cannot manage. For example, if we just do not want to attend the dorm meeting early on Saturday morning, we might give this excuse: "I have been fighting off a cold all week, and I need to sleep on Saturday morning. I will be sure to attend the next meeting." This type of lie also occurs frequently in writing class. A student with weak writing skills sometimes asks a friend to write a composition for him or her. When the teacher confronts the student, the student almost always denies the accusation. When we do not want to admit the truth and then face the consequences, we use lies to <u>avoid</u> difficulties.

4   In contrast, we sometimes tell a white lie when we do not want to hurt someone else's feelings. For example, if a good friend shows up with an <u>unflattering</u> new haircut,

EXAMPLE ESSAY

we could be truthful and say, "That haircut looks awful. It does not <u>suit</u> you at all!" Instead, we are more likely to lie and say, "I like your haircut. It looks good on you," and spare our friend's feelings. These types of lies are generally not considered negative or wrong. In fact, many people who have told the truth to loved ones, only to see a negative reaction, wish they *had* told a white lie. Therefore, white lies can be useful in maintaining good relationships.

5 Similarly, we tell "protective lies" in order to help us get out of or avoid dangerous situations. Parents, particularly those with young children, may teach their children to use this type of lie in certain circumstances. What should children do if a stranger calls while the parents are out? Good parents have told their children to explain that Mom and Dad are too busy to come to the phone at that time. In this situation, protective lying may prevent harm or disaster.

6 People lie for many reasons, both good and bad. However, before we <u>resort to</u> lying to cover up mistakes or to avoid unpleasant situations, perhaps we should rethink our motives for lying. We never know when our lies might be exposed and cause us embarrassment or the loss of people's trust.

puppet: a toy that is moved by strings

blunders: careless mistakes

avoid: to keep away from

yield: to produce

unflattering: not favorable

suit: to be appropriate; to fit properly

resort to: to do something only because other options have failed

3. What is the thesis statement?

_____

_____

4. What three examples of liars does the author give in the introduction paragraph?

a. _____

b. _____

c. _____

5. Supporting sentences: In paragraph 5, the author supports the topic sentence by giving an example of a dangerous situation. What example does the author give?

_____

_____

6. Reread the concluding paragraph of "Why Do We Lie?" Does the writer offer **a suggestion, an opinion,** or **a prediction**? Circle the appropriate phrase in bold type and write the final sentence from the essay.

_____

_____

_____

_____

Building Better Sentences

Correct and varied sentence structure is essential to the quality of your essay. For further practice with "Why Do We Lie?" go to Practice 15 on page 156 in Appendix 2.

Activity 2   **Studying an Example Essay**

Read and study the following essay. Work with a partner to answer the questions before and after the essay. These questions will help you understand the content and the organization of the essay.

Essay 16

This cause-effect essay discusses some of the effects of the breakup of the Soviet Union.

1. Do you remember the fall of the Soviet Union?

2. In your opinion, what is the best form of government?

The Fall

1 For almost fifty years, the Cold War was one of the most talked about issues in politics. Tensions between NATO countries and the Soviet Union were high, and the world felt the <u>potential</u> danger of a disastrous conflict. When the Iron Curtain fell, many countries <u>rejoiced</u>. Independent-minded Soviet Republics got the independence they had wanted, and the communist <u>ideology</u> that had been so <u>prevalent</u> began <u>to lose ground.</u> More than ten years after the break-up of the Soviet Union, the effects are still being felt.

2 One of the most obvious changes in the post-communist world is the <u>shift</u> to a market economy. Governments that had normally <u>subsidized</u> prices for their consumers—for things like food, transportation, and housing and electricity—are now letting competition and external factors set prices. Inflation is high, and many citizens are having a difficult time adjusting to the <u>fluctuations</u> in prices based on supply and demand. However, imported goods are now commonplace in local markets, so consumers have more choices in what they buy. The <u>switch</u> to a market economy is often a painful process, but the citizens of the former Soviet Union are still confident that they will one day benefit financially from the economic changes.

3 Another anticipated effect of the fall of the Iron Curtain is <u>sovereignty</u>. The Soviet Union existed as one entity for many years, but now one can count thirteen newly formed republics. These republics are currently in the process of shaping their own identities. They can focus on rebuilding their own cultures, languages, and priorities. This empowerment increases national pride and uniqueness. The idea of all Soviets being one and the same is now gone. National identity is at the <u>forefront</u> of many people's minds.

4 While many former Soviets now feel a sense of national identity, the fall of the Soviet Union has taken away the identity of many others. Many ethnic groups have lived in this part of the world for generations. They were raised as Soviets, spoke Russian as a native language, and were taught to believe that they were citizens of the great superpower. Koreans, Tartars, Uighurs, and others can be found in most of the former Soviet Republics. Now that independence has spread from Eastern Europe to Central Asia, many of these citizens are considered minority groups. They do not want to be <u>repatriated</u> to distant lands such as North Korea or China. While they look Korean or Chinese, they do not speak the languages and have not had ties with these parts of the world for many years. As the newly formed republics try to <u>reinvigorate</u> their traditions and values, many of the ethnic minorities tend to feel left out with no place to really call home.

5 The fall of the Soviet Union is perhaps one of the most <u>momentous</u> events of the twentieth Century. Walls fell, markets opened, and people rejoiced in the streets, anticipating a life full of opportunities and freedom to make their own choices. A system that took so long to build will probably need as much time, if not more, to truly adapt to the free enterprise system that is now the world model.

potential: possible

rejoice: celebrate

ideology: beliefs

prevalent: common; accepted

to lose ground: become unpopular; weaken

fluctuation: movement or change

switch: change

sovereignty: self-government; supremacy

forefront: leading edge; vanguard

repatriate: to send people back to their original homeland

shift: change

subsidize : finance; support

reinvigorate: to revitalize, bring back to life

momentous: important; eventful

3. What is the writer's main message in this essay?

_____

_____

4. In a few words, what is the general topic of "The Fall"?

_____

5. The writer presents several effects of the breakup of the Soviet Union. What type of organization does the writer use in this essay?

_____

_____

6. Reread the thesis statement of "The Fall." Are the specific effects of the fall of the Soviet Union mentioned **(stated),** or is the thesis general **(implied)?**

_____

7. Supporting sentences: In paragraph 2, the writer explains that one effect of the Soviet breakup is the new market economy. What examples does the writer give to show that countries are now in a market economy?

_____

_____

8. Supporting sentences: In paragraph 4, the author writes about ethnic minorities and their problems. Which minorities are specifically mentioned and what problems are they having?

_____

_____

Building Better Sentences

Correct and varied sentence structure is essential to the quality of your essay. For further practice with "The Fall," go to Practice 16 on page 157 in Appendix 2.

DEVELOPING CAUSE-EFFECT ESSAYS

In this next section, you will work on cause-effect essays as you make an outline, write supporting information, study connectors, and choose a topic. Practicing these skills will help you write an effective cause-effect essay.

Activity 3   **Outlining Practice**

The two outlines that follow show the causes and effects of teen drug abuse. The first one outlines the causes (focus-on-causes method) and the second one outlines the effects (focus-on-effects method) of teen drug abuse. Complete the outlines with a partner. Use your imagination, knowledge of the topic, and understanding of essay organization. (See Unit 1 for a review of the structure of an essay.) Be sure to notice the thesis statements and use them to help you complete the outlines.

FOCUS-ON-CAUSES OUTLINE

TOPIC: The causes of teenage drug abuse

I. Introduction (paragraph 1)

Thesis statement: Teen drug abuse can occur for many reasons, some of which are _____

_____

_____

_____

II. Body

    A. Paragraph 2 (cause 1) topic sentence: Teens often begin using drugs because of low

       self-esteem.

SUPPORT

       1. Teens are sensitive during adolescence.

       2. Drugs make teens feel powerful.

       3. _____

    B. Paragraph 3 (cause 2) topic sentence: _____

       _____

SUPPORT

       1. In many families, both parents work outside the home.

       2. Parents often don't have time to pay attention to their children's needs.

       3. Parents may not be aware of the warning signs that their children show.

    C. Paragraph 4 (cause 3) topic sentence: _____

       _____

SUPPORT

       1. They want to be seen as "cool."

       2. They want to fit into a group.

       3. They want "instant" friends.

III. Conclusion (paragraph 5) (restated thesis): _____

    _____

The best way to stop teens from using and abusing drugs is to address all these causes. Only then
will there be a decrease in the number of teenagers who use drugs.

5. Topic sentence: Paragraphs 2, 3, and 4 each give a reason for requiring school uniforms. These reasons can be found in the topic sentence of each paragraph. What are the reasons?

   Paragraph 2: _____

   Paragraph 3: _____

   Paragraph 4: _____

6. Supporting sentences: In paragraph 4, what supporting information does the writer give to show that uniforms make students equal?

   _____

   _____

   _____

7. Which paragraph presents a counterargument (an argument that is contrary to, or the opposite of, the writer's opinion)? What is the counterargument?

   _____

   _____

   _____

8. The writer gives a refutation of the counterargument (shows that it is wrong). What is the writer's refutation?

   _____

   _____

   _____

9. Write the sentence from the concluding paragraph of "The School Uniform Question" that restates the thesis.

   _____

   _____

   _____

10. Reread the concluding paragraph. What is the writer's opinion about this issue?

_____

_____

_____

Building Better Sentences

Correct and varied sentence structure is essential to the quality of your essay. For further practice with "The School Uniform Question," go to Practice 19 on page 160 in Appendix 2.

COUNTERARGUMENT AND REFUTATION

The key to persuading the reader that your viewpoint is valid is to support it in every paragraph. While this is not a problem in the first few paragraphs of your essay, the counterargument goes against your thesis statement. This is why every counterargument that you include in your essay needs a refutation. A refutation is a response to the counterargument that disproves it.

Look at the following excerpts from two argumentative essays in this chapter. The counterarguments are in italics and the refutations are underlined.

Essay 19:

Opponents of mandatory uniforms say that students who wear school uniforms cannot express their individuality. This point has some merit on the surface. <u>However, as stated previously, school is a place to learn, not to flaunt wealth and fashion.</u>

Essay 21:

> *The opponents of capital punishment might say that no one has the right to decide who should die, including the government.* <u>However, when the government sends soldiers to war, it is deciding the fate of those soldiers who will die. As long as the government has a right to send its citizens to a battlefield, it has a right to put criminals to death.</u>

As you can see, what begins as a counterargument ends up as another reason in support of your opinion.

On the Web
Try Unit 5
Activity 3

WRITER'S NOTE: Arguing Your Point of View

Imagine that you are having an argument with a friend about your topic. He disagrees with your opinion. What do you think will be his strongest argument against your point of view? How will you respond to this counterargument? (Your answer is your refutation.)

DEVELOPING ARGUMENTATIVE ESSAYS

In this next section, you will work on argumentative essays as you make an outline, write supporting information, study modals, and choose a topic.

OUTLINING

Activity 2   **Outlining Practice**

The following outline, which is designed for an argumentative essay, is missing some supporting information. Work with a partner to complete the outline. Use your imagination, knowledge of the topic, and understanding of essay organization to complete this outline with your partner. After you finish, compare your supporting information with that of other students.

Topic: Mandatory physical education in school

I. Introduction (paragraph 1)
Thesis statement: Physical education classes should be required for all public school students in all grades.

II. Body

    A. Paragraph 2 (pro argument 1) topic sentence: Physical education courses promote children's general health.

        1. Researchers have proved that exercise has maximum benefit if done regularly.

        2. _____

        3. Students should learn the importance of physical fitness at an early age.

    B. Paragraph 3 (pro argument 2) topic sentence: Physical education teaches children transferable life skills.

        1. Kids learn about teamwork while playing team sports.

        2. Kids learn about the benefits of healthy competition.

        3. _____

    C. Paragraph 4 (pro argument 3) topic sentence: _____

_____

        1. Trained physical education teachers can teach more effectively than parents.

        2. Physical education teachers can usually point a student toward the sport that is more appropriate.

        3. Schools generally have the appropriate facilities and equipment.

    D. Paragraph 5 (counterargument and refutation)

        1. Counterargument: Some parents might disagree and claim that only academic subjects be taught in school.

        2. Refutation: Most parents don't have time or resources to see to it that their children are getting enough exercise. Therefore, it becomes the school's duty to ensure that children are healthy in both mind and body.

SUPPORT

SUPPORT

SUPPORT

III. Conclusion (paragraph 6) (restated thesis): _____

_____ (opinion) Physical education has often

been downplayed as a minor part of daily school life. If its benefits are taken into account and if

schools adopt a twelve-year fitness plan, the positive results will foster a new awareness of not

only physical fitness but also communications skills.

ADDING SUPPORTING INFORMATION

Activity 3 — Supporting Information

The following argumentative essay is missing the supporting information. As you read the essay, work with a partner to write supporting sentences for each paragraph. If you need more space, use a separate piece of paper. After you finish, compare your supporting information with that of other students.

Essay 20

Do you know anyone who owns a gun?

No More Guns

EXAMPLE ESSAY

1 The year 1774 was pivotal in the history of the United States. It marked the beginning of the Revolutionary War, which lasted thirteen years and claimed thousands of lives. Fighting against the British, the Americans had to rely on individual citizens because they did not have a well-organized army. As farmers and hunters, many citizens already owned guns. These rifles proved indispensable in defeating the British. After the war, citizens were reluctant to give up their rifles, as they feared future invasions. Because of this fear, an amendment was added to the Constitution of the United States guaranteeing citizens the right to bear arms. Times have changed, however. The United States has one of the largest military forces in the world, and Americans are no longer called upon to use their own weapons in the military. Although people no longer need guns for this purpose, there are in fact over 200,000,000 guns in circulation. Unfortunately, gun-related deaths continue to increase every year, with many innocent people losing their lives. Despite the original intention of the Second Amendment, the United States would be much better off if ownership of guns by private citizens was outlawed.

2 The first benefit of making guns illegal is that the number of accidental shootings would decrease.

_____

_____

_____

3 Another benefit of outlawing guns is that the streets would be safer.

_____

_____

_____

4 If guns were illegal, people would be less likely to harm loved ones in moments of anger.

_____

_____

_____

5 Some people say that they feel safer having a gun at home. However, if guns were more difficult to own, fewer criminals would have them. Fewer guns would lead to a decrease in the number of gun-related crimes and victims.

_____

_____

_____

6 Statistics show that the occurrence of violent crime is much lower in countries that do not allow citizens to carry weapons. Although it is doubtful that the United States would ever completely outlaw the private ownership of weapons, wouldn't it be nice to lower the risk of being shot? It is time for the United States to take a close look at its antiquated gun laws and make some changes for the safety of its citizens.

Building Better Sentences

Correct and varied sentence structure is essential to the quality of your essay.
For further practice with "No More Guns," go to Practice 20 on page 161 in
Appendix 2.

WRITER'S NOTE: Modals and Tone

Use modals to soften your verbs. For example, change "The president *must* change his policy" (too strong) to "The president *should* change his policy" (softer).

LANGUAGE FOCUS: Controlling Tone with Modals

In argumentative essays, good writers are aware of how their arguments sound. Are they too strong? Not strong enough? Certain words can help control the tone of your argument.

Asserting a Point

Strong modals such as *must*, *had better*, and *should* help writers to assert their main points. When you use these words, readers know where you stand on an issue.

Examples:

The facts clearly show that researchers <u>must</u> stop unethical animal testing.

People who value their health <u>had better</u> stop smoking now.

Public schools <u>should</u> require uniforms in order to benefit both the students and society as a whole.

Acknowledging an Opposing Point

Weaker modals such as *may*, *might*, *could*, *can*, and *would* help writers make an opposing opinion sound weak. You acknowledge an opposing point when you use *may*, for example, but this weak modal shows that the statement is not strong and can be refuted.

Examples:

While it <u>may</u> be true that people have eaten meat for a long time, the number one killer of Americans now is heart disease, caused in part by the consumption of large amounts of animal fat.

Some Americans <u>may</u> be against legalizing same-sex marriages, but many people were against interracial marriages at first, too.

On the Web
Try Unit 5
Activity 4

WRITER'S NOTE: Using Modals for Assertion and for Acknowledging an Opposing View

You are probably already familiar with most of the modals in English—*may, might, can, could, would, must, should, had better, ought to*. Modals can be useful in argumentative essays for two reasons: strong modals help writers make their opinions sound stronger, and weak modals make opposing views sound weaker.

| Activity 4 | Choosing Modals |

Read the following argumentative essay. Underline the modal in parentheses that you feel is most appropriate.

Essay 21

Life or Death?

1   How would you feel if a loved one were killed? Would you want retribution, or would sending the killer to prison be enough? This question has been asked many times, but people are not in agreement about the ultimate punishment. We all know that it is wrong to take a human life, but if our government does the killing, is it still a crime? Some people say that the government does not have the right to end someone's life, but the following reasons (*might/will*) show why capital punishment should be preserved.

2   The first reason for allowing the death penalty is for the sake of punishment itself. Most people agree that criminals who commit serious crimes (*might/should*) be separated from society. The punishment (*will/ought to*) depend on the degree of the crime. Capital punishment, the most severe form of punishment, ends criminals' lives. It seems reasonable that this severe punishment be reserved for those who commit the most serious crimes.

3   The second reason to preserve capital punishment is financial. The government (*should, does*) not have to spend a lot of money on criminals. Next to capital punishment, the most severe punishment is a life sentence in prison, where the government (*might/has to*) take care of criminals until they die naturally. These criminals do not work, but they receive free housing and food. It is unfair to use tax dollars for such a purpose.

EXAMPLE ESSAY

EXAMPLE ESSAY

4 The last reason for continuing the use of the death penalty is based on the purpose of government. If the government has legitimate power to make, judge, and carry out the laws, it (*may/should*) also have the power to decide if criminals should die. Capital punishment is like any other sentence. If one believes that the government has the right to charge a fine or put criminals into jail, then the government (*could/must*) also have the same power to decide the fate of a prisoner's life.

5 The opponents of capital punishment (*must/might*) say that nobody has the right to decide who should die, including the government. However, when the government sends soldiers into war, in some way, it is deciding those soldiers' fate; some will live and some will be killed. As long as the government has a right to send its citizens to a battlefield, it has a right to put criminals to death.

6 There are many good reasons to preserve capital punishment. Certainly not every criminal (*can/should*) be put to death. Capital punishment (*ought to/will*) be viewed as the harshest form of punishment. If no punishment (*can/should*) reform a murderer, then capital punishment is the best thing that can be done for that person and for society.

Building Better Sentences

Correct and varied sentence structure is essential to the quality of your essay. For further practice with "Life or Death?" go to Practice 21 on page 162 in Appendix 2.

CHOOSING A TOPIC

Activity 5 | **Writing Pro and Con Thesis Statements**

Read the following list of topics for argumentative essays. For each topic, write a pro (for) thesis statement and a con (against) thesis statement related to the topic. Then compare your statements with your classmates' statements.

Example:

Topic: Women in the military

> Pro thesis statement: <u>In a society where women are chief executive officers of companies, leaders of nations, and family breadwinners, there is no reason why they should not play an active role in the military.</u>

> Con thesis statement: <u>Women should not be allowed to fight in the military because they do not have the strength or endurance required in combat.</u>

1. TOPIC: Using animals in disease research

   Pro thesis statement: _____

_____

Con thesis statement: _____

_____

2. TOPIC: Homeschooling

Pro thesis statement: _____

_____

Con thesis statement: _____

_____

3. TOPIC: Space exploration

Pro thesis statement: _____

_____

Con thesis statement: _____

_____

4. TOPIC: Smoking in public buildings

Pro thesis statement: _____

_____

Con thesis statement: _____

_____

AVOIDING FAULTY LOGIC

**On the Web
Try Unit 5
Activity 5**

Good writers want to convince readers to agree with their arguments—their reasons and conclusions. If your arguments are not logical, readers won't be convinced. Logic can help prove your point and disprove your opponent's point—and perhaps change a reader's mind about an issue. If you use faulty logic (logic not based on fact), readers will not believe you or take your position seriously.

This section presents a few logical errors that writers sometimes make in argumentative essays. Try to avoid these errors in your writing.

Sweeping Generalizations

Words such as *all*, *always*, and *never* are too broad and can't be supported.

> Example: *All* Americans eat fast food.

> Problem: Maybe every American that you know eats fast food, but the statement that ALL Americans eat it can't be proven.

Events Related Only by Sequence

When one event happens, it doesn't necessarily cause a second event to happen, even if one follows the other in time.

> Example: Henry went to the football game, then he got drunk. Therefore, football games cause drunkenness.

> Problem: The two events may have happened in that order, but don't mislead the reader into thinking that the first action was responsible for the second.

Inappropriate Authority Figures

Using famous names may often help you prove or disprove your point. However, be sure to use the name logically and in the proper context.

> Example: Madonna is a good singer. As a result, she would make a good orchestra conductor.

> Problem: While Madonna may be a good singer, this quality will not necessarily make her a good orchestra conductor.

Hasty Generalizations

Hasty generalizations are just what they sound like—making quick judgments based on inadequate information. This kind of logical fallacy is a common error in argumentative writing.

> Example: Joe didn't want to study at a university. Instead, he decided to go to a technical school. He is now making an excellent salary repairing computers. Bill doesn't want to study at a university. Therefore, he should go to a technical school to become financially successful.

> Problem: While Joe and Bill have something in common (they don't want to study at a university), this fact alone does not mean that Bill would be successful doing the same thing that Joe did. Other information may be important as well, such as the fact that Joe has lots of experience with computers or that Bill has problems with manual dexterity.

Loaded Words

Some words contain positive or negative connotations. Try to avoid them when you make an argument.

Example: The blue-flag *freedom fighters* won the war against the green-flag *guerrillas*.

Problem: The words *freedom fighters* (positive) and *guerrillas* (negative) may bias readers about the two groups without any support for the bias.

Either/Or Arguments

When you argue a point, be careful not to limit the choices to only two or three.

Example: The instructor must either return the tests or dismiss the class.

Problem: This statement implies that only two choices are available to the instructor.

Activity 6	Faulty Logic

Read the following paragraph and underline all the uses of faulty logic. Write the kind of error above the words.

Next week our fine upstanding citizens will go to the polls to vote for or against a penny sales tax for construction of a new stadium. This law, if passed, will cause extreme hardship for local residents. Our taxes are high enough as it is, so why do our city's apathetic leaders think that we will run happily to the polls and vote YES? If we take a look at what happened to our sister city as a result of a similar bill, we will see that this new tax will have negative effects. Last year that city raised its sales tax by 1 percent. Only three weeks later, the city was nearly destroyed by a riot in the streets. If we want to keep our fair city as it is, we must either vote NO on the ballot question or live in fear of violence.

IDEAS
BRAINSTORMING

Brainstorming will help you get started with your argumentative essay. In this section, you will choose any method of brainstorming that works for you and develop supporting information.

Activity 7 — Choosing a Topic

1. First, choose a thesis from the statements that you wrote in Activity 5 on pages 121–122 or choose any other topic and thesis statement that you want to write about. Remember that the topic must have more than one point of view to qualify as an argument.

   Essay topic: _____

   Thesis statement: _____

   _____

2. Now brainstorm about your topic. Write everything you can think of that supports your argument. Use clustering, diagramming, or another method of brainstorming. You may want to begin by answering this question about your thesis statement: *Why do I believe this?*

3. Look at your brainstorming information again. Choose three or four reasons that support your thesis *most effectively* and circle them. You now know what your major supporting information will be.

4. Now that you have written your thesis and a few reasons to support it, it's time to give attention to opposing points of view. On the lines below, write one counterargument and a refutation for your argumentative essay.

   Counterargument: _____

   _____

   _____

   Refutation: _____

   _____

   _____

   Remember that in your conclusion, you should include a restatement of the thesis and your opinion about the issue.

Activity 8 — Planning with an Outline

Complete the outline on page 126 as a guide to help you brainstorm a more detailed plan for your argumentative essay. Use your ideas from Activity 7 (above). You may need to use either more or fewer points under each heading. Write complete sentences where possible.

TOPIC: _____

   I. Introduction (paragraph 1)

     A. Hook: _____

     B. Connecting information: _____

        _____

     C. Thesis statement: _____

        _____

   II. Body

     A. Paragraph 2 (first reason) topic sentence: _____

        _____

SUPPORT

         1. _____

         2. _____

         3. _____

     B. Paragraph 3 (second reason) topic sentence: _____

        _____

SUPPORT

         1. _____

         2. _____

         3. _____

     C. Paragraph 4 (third reason) topic sentence: _____

        _____

SUPPORT

         1. _____

         2. _____

         3. _____

D. Paragraph 4 (counterargument and refutation)

SUPPORT

1. Counterargument: _____

_____

2. Refutation: _____

_____

III. Conclusion (paragraph 5)

A. Restated thesis: _____

_____

B. Opinion: _____

_____

Activity 9 — Peer Editing Your Outline

Exchange outlines with another student. Read each other's outlines and make comments using Peer Editing Sheet 7 on page 197.

Activity 10 — Writing an Argumentative Essay

After you have read your classmate's review of your outline, think about any changes you want to make in your essay. Make sure you have enough information to develop your supporting sentences. Then write your argumentative essay. Save all your work, including your brainstorming notes, revised drafts, and the Peer Editing Sheet. Be sure to refer to the seven steps in the writing process in Appendix 1 on page 000.

Activity 11 — Peer Editing Your Essay

Exchange argumentation essays from Activity 10 with a partner. Then use Peer Editing Sheet 8 on page 199 to help you comment on your partner's paper. It is important to offer positive comments that will help the writer.

TOPICS FOR WRITING

| Activity 12 | Essay Writing Practice |

Here are more ideas for topics for an argumentative essay. Before you write, be sure to refer to the seven steps in the writing process in Appendix 1.

1. The media often place heavy emphasis on the opinions and actions of celebrities such as actors and sports stars. Should we pay attention to these opinions and actions? Are they important or not? Choose one side and write your essay in support of it.

2. At what age should a person be considered an adult? Make a decision about this issue, then argue your point of view. Don't forget to include a counterargument and refutation.

3. Consider the issue of assisted suicide for terminally ill people. Do you think it should be allowed? Argue one side or the other of this issue.

4. Should a passing TOEFL score be the main requirement for international students to enter a university? What are the pros and cons of this issue? Choose one side and write your essay in support of it.

5. Is daycare beneficial for children under the age of five? Should one parent stay home with children for the first few years of life? Develop a thesis statement about some aspect of the daycare versus home care issue and support it in your argumentative essay.

Appendixes

130

Appendix 6   Peer Editing Sheets

Appendix 7   Answer Key

Understanding the Writing Process: The Seven Steps

This section can be read at any time during the course. You will want to refer to these seven steps many times as you write your essays.

THE ASSIGNMENT

Imagine that you have been given the following assignment: *Write an essay in which you discuss the benefits or problems of vegetarianism*. What should you do first? What should you do second, and so on? There are many ways to write, but most good writers follow certain general steps in the writing process. These steps are guidelines that are not always followed in order.

Look at this list of steps. Which ones do you do? Which ones have you never done?

1. Choosing a topic (Remember your audience.)

2. Brainstorming

3. Outline and rough draft

4. Cleaning up the rough draft

5. Peer editing

6. Revising the draft

7. Proofing the final paper

Next you will see how one student, Sean, went through the steps to do the assignment. First, read the final essay that Sean gave his teacher.

Essay 22

Better Living as a Vegetarian

1   The hamburger is an American cultural icon that is known all over the world. Eating meat, especially beef, is an integral part of daily life for a majority of people in the United States. The consumption of large quantities of meat is a major contributing factor toward a great many deaths in this country, including the unnecessarily high number of deaths

131

EXAMPLE WRITING

from heart-related problems. Though it has caught on slowly in this culture, vegetarianism is a way of life that can help improve not only the quality of people's lives but also their longevity.

2 Surprising as it may sound, vegetarianism can have beneficial effects on the environment. Because demand for meat animals is so high, cattle are being raised in areas where rain forests once stood. As rain forest land is cleared in order to make room for cattle ranches, the environmental balance is upset. This could have serious consequences for humans. Studies show that much of the current global warming is due to disturbing the rain forests.

3 More important at an individual level is the question of how eating meat affects a person's health. Meat, unlike vegetables, can contain very large amounts of fat. Eating this fat has been connected in research cases with certain kinds of cancer. If people cut down on the amounts of meat they ate, they would automatically be lowering their risks of disease. Furthermore, eating animal fat can lead to obesity, and obesity can cause numerous health problems. For example, obesity can cause people to slow down and their heart to have to work harder. This results in high blood pressure. Meat is also high in cholesterol, and this only adds to health problems. With so much fat consumption in this country, it is no wonder that heart disease is a leading killer of Americans.

4 If people followed vegetarian diets, they would not only be healthier but also live longer. Eating certain kinds of vegetables, such as broccoli, brussels sprouts, and cauliflower, has been shown to reduce the chance of contracting colon cancer later in life. Vegetables do not contain the "bad" fats that meat does. Vegetables do not contain cholesterol, either. Furthermore, native inhabitants of areas of the world where people eat more vegetables than meat, notably certain areas of the former Soviet Asian republics, routinely live to be over one hundred.

5 Some people argue that, human nature being what it is, it would be unhealthy for humans to not eat meat. They say that humans are naturally carnivores and cannot help wanting to consume a juicy piece of red meat. However, anthropologists have shown that early humans ate meat only when other foods were not abundant. Man is inherently a herbivore, not a carnivore.

6 Numerous scientific studies have shown the benefits of vegetarianism for people in general, and I know firsthand how my life has improved since I decided to give up meat entirely. Though it was difficult at first, I have never regretted my decision to become a vegetarian. I feel better, and my friends tell me that I look better than ever before. More and more people are becoming aware of the risks associated with meat consumption. If you become vegetarian, your life will improve, too.

STEPS IN THE WRITING PROCESS

STEP 1: CHOOSING A TOPIC

For this assignment, the topic was given: the benefits or problems of vegetarianism. As you consider the assignment, you have to decide what kind of essay to write. Will you compare or contrast the benefits of vegetarianism with another type of diet? Will you talk about the causes and effects of vegetarianism? Will you argue that vegetarianism is or is not better than eating animal products?

Sean chose to write an argumentative essay about vegetarianism to try to convince readers of its benefits. The instructor had explained that this essay was to be serious in nature and have solid facts to back up the claims made.

STEP 2: BRAINSTORMING

The next step for Sean was to brainstorm.

In this step, you write every idea that pops into your head about your topic. Some of these ideas will be good, and some will be bad; write them all. The main purpose of brainstorming is to write as many ideas as you can think of. If one idea looks especially good, you might circle that idea or put a check next to it. If you write an idea and you know right away that you are not going to use it, you can cross it out.

Brainstorming methods include making lists, clustering (see Unit 2), and diagramming (see Unit 3). Use whatever method you like best.

Look at Sean's brainstorming diagram on the topic of vegetarianism.

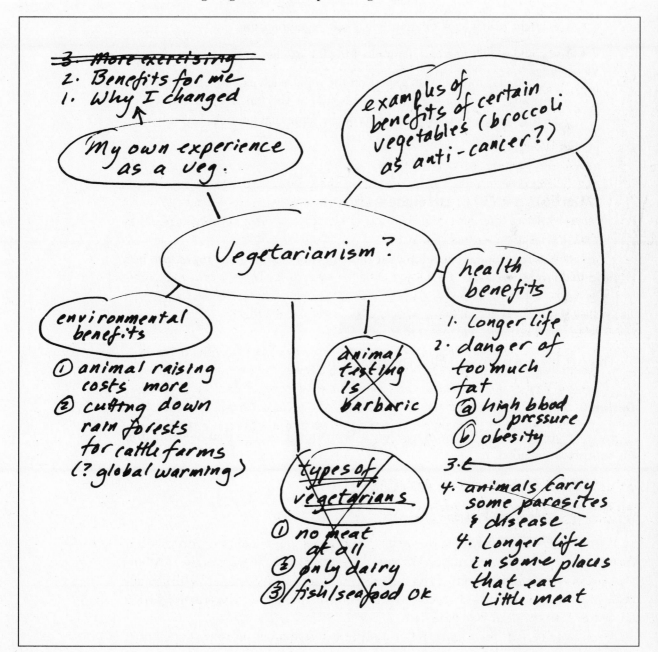

Sean's brainstorming diagram

As you can see from the brainstorming diagram, Sean considered many benefits of being a vegetarian. Notice a few items in the diagram. As he organized his brainstorming, Sean wrote "examples of benefits of certain vegetables" as a spoke on the wheel. Then he realized that this point would be a good number 3 in the list of benefits, so he drew an arrow to show that he should move it there. For number 4, Sean wrote "animals carry some parasites and disease." Then he decided that this is not related to the topic of the benefits of becoming a vegetarian, so he crossed it out.

Getting the Information

How would you get the information for this brainstorming exercise?

- You might read a book or an article about vegetarianism.

- You could spend time in a library looking for articles on the subject.

- You could also interview an expert on the topic, such as a vegetarian or a nutritionist. This method is not only useful but also fun. You can ask the person specific questions about parts of the topic that are not clear to you.

WRITER'S NOTE: Do Research

To get information and develop your thoughts about your essay topic, you may need to do some research.

STEP 3: OUTLINE AND ROUGH DRAFT

This step has two parts: an outline and a rough draft.

Outline

Next, create an outline for the essay. Here is Sean's rough outline that he wrote from his brainstorming notes.

I. Introduction
   a. Define vegetarianism
   b. List different types

   c. Thesis statement: _____

II. Environmental benefits
   a. Rain forests
   b. Global warming

III. Health issues

    a. Too much fat from meat → obesity → diseases → cancer

    b. High blood pressure and heart disease

    c. Cancer-fighting properties of broccoli and cauliflower, etc.

IV. Counterargument

    a. Man is carnivore?

    b. Not true

V. Conclusion

    Opinion: life will improve

After you have chosen the main points for your essay, you will need to develop some supporting details. You should include examples, reasons, explanations, definitions, or personal experiences. One of the most common techniques in generating these supporting details is asking specific questions about the topic, for example:

SUPPORT

What is it?

What happened?

How did this happen?

What is it like or not like? Why?

Rough Draft

Next, Sean wrote a rough draft. As Sean wrote each paragraph of his essay, he paid careful attention to the language he used. He chose a formal sentence structure including a variety of sentence types. In addition, his sentences varied in length, with the average sentence containing almost twenty words. (Sentences in conversation tend to be very short; sentences in academic writing tend to be longer.) Sean also took great care in choosing appropriate vocabulary. In addition to specific terminology such as "obesity," "blood pressure," and "consumption," he avoided the conversational "you" in the topic sentences of paragraphs 4 and 5 when he referred to "people" and "humans."

In this step you take information from your brainstorming session and write the essay. This first draft may contain many errors, such as misspellings, incomplete ideas, and comma errors. At this point, don't worry about correcting the errors. The main thing is to put your ideas into sentences.

You may feel that you don't know what you think about the topic yet. In this case, it may be difficult for you to write, but it's important to just write, no matter what comes out. Sometimes writing helps you think, and as soon as you form a new thought, you can write it.

Better Living as a Vegetarian

Wow - too abrupt? You don't talk about hamburgers any more??

(Do you like hamburgers?) Eating meat, especially beef, is an interesting part of the daily

vocabulary?

life in the United States. In addition, this high eating of meat is a major contributing thing *factor*

word choice?

causes

that makes a great many deaths in this country, including the unnecessarily high number

of deaths from heart-related problems. Vegetarianism has caught on slowly in this culture.

) and it

Vegetarianism is a way of life that can help improve not only the quality of people's lives but

also people's longevity.   → *the quality but also the length of people's lives*

This is not a topic sentence   Because demand for meat animals is so high, Cattle are being raised in areas where the

rain forest once stood. As rain forest land is cleared in massive amounts in order to make

room for the cattle ranches, the environmental balance is being upset. This could have

For example,   *transition?*

serious consequences for us in both the near and long term. How much of the current global

warming is due to man's disturbing the rain forest?

You need a more specific topic relating to health.

(Meat contains a high amount of fat.) Eating this fat has been connected in research

cases with certain kinds of cancer. Furthermore, eating animal fat can lead to obesity, and

obesity can cause many different kinds of diseases, for example, obesity can cause people to

slow down and their heart to have to word harder. This results in high blood pressure.

Meat is high in cholesterol, and this only adds to the health problems. With the high

consumption of animal fat in this country, it is no wonder that heart disease is a leading

killer of Americans.

On the other hand, eating a vegetarian diet can improve a person's health. And

Sean's rough draft

Practice 16   "The Fall", page 90

A. (paragraph 1)

1. Tensions between two groups were high.

2. The two groups were the NATO countries and the Soviet Union.

3. The world felt a potential danger.

4. The danger was of a disastrous conflict.

_____

_____

B. (paragraph 2)

1. One of the most obvious changes is the shift.

2. The change occurred in the post-communist world.

3. The change is to a market economy.

_____

_____

C. (paragraph 3)

1. These republics are in a process.

2. This process is current.

3. They are shaping something.

4. It is their own identities.

_____

_____

D. (paragraph 4)

1. They do not want to be repatriated to lands.

2. The lands are distant.

3. There are lands such as North Korea or China.

_____

_____

Practice 17   "Television at Its Worst", page 96

A. (paragraph 1)

  1. Mr. Stevenson has just come home from somewhere.

  2. He came from work.

  3. He had a terribly tiring day there.

  _____

  _____

B. (paragraph 1)

  1. People use television for some reasons.

  2. They use television to relax.

  3. They use television to forget about troubles.

  4. The troubles occur daily.

  _____

  _____

C. (paragraph 3)

  1. There is another negative point about TV watching.

  2. It may cause children to have difficulty distinguishing between some things.

  3. They don't know what's real.

  4. They don't know what's not real.

  _____

  _____

D. (paragraph 5)

  1. Television has changed over the years.

  2. It now includes more and more programs.

  3. These programs are inappropriate for children.

  _____

  _____

Practice 18   "Effects of Computers on Higher Education", page 98

A. (paragraph 2)

1. We are now able to sit down in front of a screen.

2. The screen is digital.

3. We can listen to a lecture.

4. The lecture is being given at another university.

_____

_____

B. (paragraph 3)

1. It is easy to use the Internet.

2. It is easy to use databases.

3. All we have to do is type in a few key words.

4. We wait a few moments.

_____

_____

C. (paragraph 4)

1. Assignments are becoming more common.

2. They are e-mail assignments.

3. They occur at universities.

_____

_____

D. (paragraph 4)

1. This is additional information.

2. We do this without using a dictionary.

3. We can write papers.

4. The papers have no spelling mistakes.

_____

_____

Practice 19   "The School Uniform Question", page 111

A. (paragraph 1)

1. All Americans believe in the right to express their opinions.

2. The opinions are their own.

3. They don't have fear.

4. The fear is punishment.

_____

_____

B. (paragraph 3)

1. Uniforms give students a message.

2. School is a special place.

3. It is a place used for learning.

_____

_____

C. (paragraph 4)

1. People's standards of living differ.

2. The differences are great.

3. Some people are well-off.

4. Others are not well-off.

_____

_____

D. (paragraph 6)

1. Studies show something about students when they wear uniforms.

2. Students learn better.

3. Students act more responsibly.

_____

_____

Practice 20   "No More Guns", page 117

A. (paragraph 1)

    1. The year was 1774.

    2. It was a pivotal year.

    3. It involved the history.

    4. The history was about the United States.

_____

_____

B. (paragraph 1)

    1. The United States has one of the largest military forces in the world.

    2. Americans are no longer called upon to use weapons.

    3. The weapons are their own.

    4. The weapons are used in the military.

_____

_____

C. (paragraph 5)

    1. Some people say something.

    2. They feel safer having a gun.

    3. The gun is at home.

_____

_____

D. (paragraph 6)

    1. There are statistics.

    2. They show that the occurrence of crime is much lower in countries.

    3. The crime is violent.

    4. The countries do not allow citizens to carry weapons.

_____

_____

Practice 21   "Life or Death", page 120

A. (paragraph 1)

1. This question has been asked many times.

2. People are not in agreement.

3. The answer is about the punishment.

4. The punishment is ultimate.

_____

_____

B. (paragraph 3)

1. There is a second reason.

2. It involves preserving capital punishment.

3. The reason is financial.

_____

_____

C. (paragraph 3)

1. These criminals do not work.

2. They receive housing.

3. They receive food.

4. These things are free.

_____

_____

D. (paragraph 6)

1. There are many reasons.

2. The reasons are good.

3. The reasons are to preserve punishment.

4. The punishment is capital.

_____

_____

APPENDIX
3

Sentence Types

English sentence structure includes three basic types of sentences: simple, compound, and complex. These types indicate how the information in the sentence is organized, not the content of the sentence. The grammatical term for a sentence is an independent clause.

SIMPLE SENTENCES

1. Simple sentences usually contain one subject and one verb.

   s   v
   Kids love television.

   v   s   v
   Does this sound like a normal routine?

2. Sometimes simple sentences can contain more than one subject or verb.

   s   v
   Brazil and the United States are large countries.

   s   v   v
   Brazil lies in South America and has a large population.

   s   v
   They were raised as Soviets,

        v
   and were taught to believe that they were citizens of the great superpower.

163

COMPOUND SENTENCES

Compound sentences are usually made up of two simple sentences (or independent clauses). Compound sentences need a *coordinating conjunction* (connector) to combine the two sentences. The most common coordinating conjunctions are

for   and   nor   but   or   yet   so

Remember that a comma is always used before the coordinating conjunction to separate the two independent clauses.

for
   S V S V
   Meagan studied hard, **for** she wanted to pass the test.

and
   S V   S V
   Meagan studied hard, **and** her classmates studied, too.

nor
   S V   S V S
   Meagan didn't study hard, **nor** did she pass the test.

but
   S V   S V
   Meagan studied hard, **but** her brother didn't study at all.

or
   S V S V
   Meagan studied hard, **or** she would have failed the test.

yet
   S V S V
   Meagan studied hard, **yet** she wasn't happy with her grade.

so
   S V S V
   Meagan studied hard, **so** the test was easy for her.

Practice 1

Study the following examples of compound sentences from the essays in this book. Draw a box around each subject, underline each verb, and circle ◯ each coordinating conjunction.

1. Brazil was colonized by Europeans, and its culture has been greatly influenced by this fact.

2. This was my first visit to the international section of the airport, and nothing was familiar.

3. Many people today are overweight, and being overweight has been connected to some kinds of cancer.

4. Walls fell, markets opened, and people rejoiced in the streets, anticipating a life full of opportunities and freedom to make their own choices.

5. Should public school students be allowed to make individual decisions about clothing, or should all students be required to wear a uniform?

6. The United States has one of the largest militaries in the world, so Americans are no longer called upon to use their own weapons in the military.

COMPLEX SENTENCES

Like compound sentences, complex sentences are made up two parts. Complex sentences, however, contain one independent clause and (at least) one dependent clause. The most common type of complex sentence uses adverb clauses.* Study the examples below.

Complex Sentences (with Adverb clauses):

The hurricane struck <u>while we were at the mall</u>.

<u>After the president gave his speech</u>, he answered most of the reporter's questions.

Adverb clauses contain subordinating conjuctions such as

while   although   after   because   if   before

Note: A more complete list of subordinating conjunctions can be found in column 3 of the Connectors chart in Appendix 5, page XX.
These subordinating conjunctions are actually part of half of a complex sentence.

Joe played tennis / after Vicky watched TV.

*The other two types of complex sentences use adjective and noun clauses.
Complex Sentences (with Adjective clauses):

A girl <u>whom I know</u> was recently accepted to Harved University.

The Eiffel Tower, <u>which is located in Paris</u>, is visited by millions of tourists annually.

Complex Sentences (with Noun clauses):

<u>What you need to do</u> is buy a new computer.

The students wanted to know <u>when their teacher would return</u>.

The word *after* is not a part by itself between the two sentences as a coordinating conjunction is in a compound sentence. Instead, the subordinating conjunction belongs grammatically to *Vicky watched TV*.

Remember that sentences beginning with these subordinating conjunctions are *dependent*. They must be attached to an independent clause. They cannot stand alone as a sentence. If they are not attached to another sentence, they are called *fragments*, or incomplete sentences. Fragments are incomplete ideas, and they cause confusion for the reader. In a complex sentence, both clauses are needed to make a complete idea so the reader can understand what you mean. Look at these examples:

Fragment   After Vicky watched TV

Complete Sentence   Joe played tennis after Vicky watched TV.

or

Complete Sentence   After Vicky watched TV, she went to bed.

Note: In compound sentences, you must put a comma at the end of the first clause. Complex sentences, however, do not need a comma if the conjunction is part of the second sentence. Study these examples:

> s   v
> Taiwanese culture puts a strong emphasis on university admission
>
> s   v
> because getting into the right university can guarantee future success.
>
> s   v   s   v
> I watched in despair as the elevator doors closed.
>
> s   v
> If the same amount of attention were given to proper diets,
>
> s
> exercise, and sunscreens, perhaps the number of overall cancer
>
> v
> cases would be reduced.

Practice 2

Study the following examples of complex sentences from the essays in this book. Draw a box ☐
around each subject, underline each verb, and circle ◯ *each subordinating conjunction.*

1. While the Northeast is experiencing snowstorms, cities like Miami, Florida, can have temperatures over 85 degrees Fahrenheit.

2. Although Brazil and the United States are unique countries, there are remarkable similarities in their size, ethnic groups, and personal values.

3. Taiwanese culture puts a strong emphasis on university admission because getting into the right university can guarantee future success.

4. If we type a grammatically incorrect sentence, one of these programs highlights the incorrect parts of the sentence and corrects them.

5. Because almost every area has a community college, students who opt to go to a community college can continue to be near their families for two more years

Additional Grammar Practice

The three essays in this section feature different grammatical errors. Each paragraph highlights one kind of error. In each case, read the entire essay before you complete the practices.

Essay 23

Remember to read the whole essay first. Then go back and complete each practice.

Practice 1   *Verb Forms*

Read the paragraph and decide whether the five underlined verbs are correct. If not, draw a line through the verb and write the correct form above the verb.

A Simple Recipe

1   "When in Rome, do as the Romans do" may <u>sound</u> ridiculous, but this proverb <u>offer</u> an important suggestion. If you travel to other countries, especially to a country that <u>is</u> very different from your own, you should <u>keeping</u> this saying in mind. For example, Japan has unique customs that <u>is</u> not found in any other country. If you <u>traveled</u> to Japan, you should find out about Japanese customs, taboos, and people beforehand.

Practice 2   *Verb Forms*

Read this paragraph carefully. Then write the correct form of the verbs in parentheses.

2   One custom is that you should (take) _____ off your shoes before

(enter) _____ someone's house. In Japan, the floor must always be kept

clean because usually people (sit) _____ , eat a meal, or even (sleep)

_____ on the floor. Another custom is giving gifts. The Japanese often

(give) _____ a small gift to people who have (do) _____

favors for them. Usually this token of gratitude (give) _____ in July and

December to keep harmonious relations with the receiver. When you (give)

_____ someone such a gift, you should make some form of apology about

it. For example, many Japanese will say, "This is just a small gift that I have for you." In

addition, it is not polite to open a gift immediately. The receiver usually (wait)

_____ until the giver has left so the giver will not be embarrassed if the

gift (turn) _____ out to be defective or displeasing.

Practice 3   *Connectors*

Read the paragraph carefully. Then fill in the blanks with one of these connectors:

because   in addition

even if   for example

first   but

3 _____ , it is important to know about Japanese taboos. All cultures have certain actions that are considered socially unacceptable. _____ something is acceptable in one culture, it can easily be taboo in another culture. _____, chopsticks are used in many cultures, _____ there are two taboos about chopsticks etiquette in Japan. _____, you should never stand the chopsticks upright in your bowl of rice. _____ standing chopsticks upright is done at a funeral ceremony, this action is associated with death. Second, you must never pass food from one pair of chopsticks to another. Again, this is related to burial rites in Japan.

Practice 4   *Articles*

There are fourteen blanks in this paragraph. Read the paragraph and write the articles a, an, *or* the *to complete the sentences. Some blanks do not require articles.*

4   Third, it is important to know that Japanese people have _____ different cultural values. One of _____ important differences in _____ cultural values is _____ Japanese desire to maintain _____ harmony at all costs. People try to avoid causing any kind of dispute. If there is _____ problem, both sides are expected to compromise in order to avoid an argument. People are expected to restrain their emotions and put _____ goal of compromise above their individual wishes. Related to this is _____ concept of patience. Japanese put _____ great deal of _____ value on _____ patience. Patience also contributes to maintaining _____ good relations with _____ everyone and avoiding _____ disputes.

Practice 5   *Prepositions*

Read this paragraph and write the correct preposition in each blank. Choose from these prepositions: into, in, to, about, with, of, around. *You may use them more than once.*

EXAMPLE WRITING

6 _____ conclusion, if you want to get along well _____

the Japanese and avoid uncomfortable situations when you go _____ Japan,

it is important to take _____ account the features _____

Japanese culture that have been discussed here. Though it may be hard to understand

Japanese customs because they are different, knowing _____ them can help

you adjust to life in Japan. If you face an unfamiliar or difficult situation when you are

_____ Japan, you should do what the people _____ you do.

In other words, "When _____ Japan, do as the Japanese do."

Essay 24

Remember to read the whole essay first. Then go back and complete each practice.

Practice 1   *Verb Forms*

Read this paragraph carefully. Then write the correct form of the verbs in parentheses.

Corporal Punishment Is Wrong

EXAMPLE WRITING

1 What should parents do when their five-year-old child says a bad word even though

the child knows it is wrong? What should a teacher (do) _____ when a

student in the second grade (call) _____ the teacher a name? When my

parents (be) _____ children forty or fifty years ago, the answer to these

questions was quite clear. The adult would spank the child immediately. Corporal

punishment (be) _____ quite common then. When I was a child, I (be)

_____ in a class in which the teacher got angry at a boy who kept

EXAMPLE WRITING

(talk) _____ after she told him to be quiet. The teacher then (shout)

_____ at the boy and, in front of all of us, (slap) _____ his

face. My classmates and I were shocked. Even after twenty years, I still remember that

incident quite clearly. If the teacher's purpose (be) _____ to (teach)

_____ us to (be) _____ quiet, she did not (succeed)

_____ . However, if her purpose was to create an oppressive mood in the

class, she succeeded. Because corporal punishment (be) _____ an

ineffective and cruel method of discipline, it should never (use) _____

under any circumstances.

Practice 2   Prepositions

Read this paragraph carefully. Write the correct preposition in each blank. Use these prepositions: in, of, for.

EXAMPLE WRITING

2 Supporters _____ corporal punishment claim that physical discipline is necessary

_____ developing a child's sense _____ personal responsibility. Justice Powell, a

former U.S. Supreme Court justice, has even said that paddling children who misbehave

has been an acceptable method _____ promoting good behavior and responsibility

_____ school children for a long time. Some people worry that stopping corporal

punishment in schools could result _____ a decline _____ school achievement.

However, just because a student stops misbehaving does not mean that he or she

suddenly has a better sense _____ personal responsibility or correct behavior.

Practice 3   Articles

Read the paragraph and write the articles a, an, or the to complete the sentences. Some blanks
do not require articles.

Writer: _____ Date: _____

Peer editor: _____

Topic: _____

1. What kind of essay will this be, cause or effect? _____ Can you tell this from the thesis statement? _____ If not, what changes can you suggest to make the purpose of the essay clearer? _____

    _____

2. Read the topic sentence for each body paragraph. Is it related to the thesis? If not, mark the topic sentences that need more work.

3. Do the supporting details relate to the topic sentences? _____ If not, which paragraph(s) need to be developed further? _____

4. The best part of the outline is _____

    _____

5. Questions I still have about the outline are _____

    _____

Writer: _____ Date: _____

Peer editor: _____

Essay title: _____

1. In a few words, what is the essay about? _____

   _____

2. Reread the introductory paragraph. Do the ideas progress smoothly from the hook to the thesis

   statement? _____ If not, what suggestions for changes would you make to the writer?

   _____

   _____

3. Do all the topic sentences support the thesis statement? _____ Mark any that do not

   and write the reason. _____

   _____

   _____

4. Look at the supporting details in each paragraph. Are they related to the topic sentence? If not,
   underline the details that need revision.

5. Check the connectors in the essay. Is it easy to understand the connection between the causes

   and effects? If not, what is missing or needs to be changed? _____

   _____

6. As you reread the essay, check for wordiness. Circle any that you find and, if you want, suggest a
   way to eliminate the wordiness.

7. Does the writer restate the thesis in the conclusion? _____ If not, bring this to the attention of the writer.

8. Compare the introduction and conclusion paragraphs. Can you see logical connections between the two? _____ If not, why not? What suggestions for improvement can you make?

_____

_____

UNIT 5, Activity 9, p. 127
Argumentative Essay Outline

Writer: _____ Date: _____

Peer editor: _____

Topic: _____

   If the answer to any of these questions is "no," tell the writer why and make any suggestions for improvement that you can think of.

   1. Is the hook interesting (does it catch the reader's attention)?   Yes   No

   2. Is the writer's opinion clear in the thesis statement?   Yes   No

   3. Do the topic sentences in the body paragraphs support the thesis?   Yes   No

   4. In each paragraph, do the supporting details relate to the topic sentence?   Yes   No

   5. Are the counterargument and refutation strong?   Yes   No

       Do they make sense?   Yes   No

   6. Does the writer restate the thesis in the conclusion?   Yes   No

   7. The best part of the outline is _____

   _____

   8. Questions I still have about the outline are _____

   _____

UNIT 5, Activity 11, p. 128
Argumentative Essay

Writer: _____ Date: _____

Peer editor: _____

Essay title: _____

1. In a few words, what is the essay about? _____

    _____

2. Reread the introductory paragraph. Do the ideas progress smoothly from the hook to the thesis

    statement? _____ If not, what suggestions for changes would you make to the writer?

    _____

    _____

3. Do all the topic sentences support the thesis statement? _____ Mark any that do not

    and write the reason. _____

    _____

    _____

4. Look at the supporting details in each paragraph. Are they related to the topic sentence? If not,
    underline the details that need revision.

5. Underline any modals. Are *must*, *had better*, or *should* used correctly to assert a point? Are *may*,
    might, *could*, *can*, or *would* used correctly to acknowledge an opposing opinion? Make suggestions
    for changes where necessary.

6. Reread the essay and look for any faulty logic. If you find any, write it here and suggest a way to

    eliminate the faulty logic. _____

_____

_____

7. Find the paragraph that contains the counterargument and refutation. Is the counterargument

stated clearly? _____ Is the refutation strong? _____ Does it make another

point in support of the writer's argument? _____ If necessary, suggest changes to the

writer to make the counterargument and refutation more effective.

8. Is the conclusion effective, that is, does it restate the thesis and the writer's opinion?

_____ If not, how can the conclusion be improved?

_____

Index